C000124875

BIRDY THE BLACK GUY FROM PORT TALBOT,SOUTH WALES

BOOK 2

◆ ◆ ◆

Nathaniel.S.Bird

◆ ◆ ◆

Paperback and e.Book written by the author

BOOK 01-Don't lose focus
BOOK 02-Just a dream
BOOK 03-You have lost the way
BOOK 04-The foolishness of folly
BOOK 05-The battle for cash
BOOK 06-The days of my life
BOOK 07-Troubles on every bend and corner
BOOK 08-Ghetto living
BOOK 09-The race has to be run
BOOK 10-The beautiful colours of life
BOOK 11-The human challenging games
BOOK 12-Actions speaks for itself
BOOK 13-Time is certainly on the move
BOOK 14-Around and around our world does spin
BOOK 15-Another day
BOOK 16-Everybody
BOOK 17-Those who are determined shall succeed
BOOK 18-You don't even know who I am
BOOK 19-You think you know it all
BOOK 20-No end to writing
BOOK 21-Chocolate dread and blue shoes
BOOK 22-Mr and Mrs Fortunate
BOOK 23-Durable treasures
BOOK 24-Our world is filled with wonders
BOOK 25-Time clock
BOOK 26-Earthly People
BOOK 27-Hopefully

◆ ◆ ◆

Index

◆ ◆ ◆

CHAPTER 1

TIME JUMP

The time jump had already started the year 1999 was already left down there in times past now even leaving behind it the year 2014 with all of it's used up days weeks with active months,it was now the year 2019 october 11th friday morning 10.57am,stephen laid there on his bed inside of his one bedroom private rented flat watching the Jeremy Vine programme on channel 5,the weather outside was showing him the chances of him seeing some sunshine today was very slim,the sky was the colour grey the roads with streets out there in the area where he lived in edmonton green were all wet with the early morning rainfall which had now stopped falling but leaving it's wet evidence all over the grey concrete grounds.

Stephen had already been out this morning quickly

going to the shopping centre to the asda store to buy a pouch of tobacco then into the one pound discount store to buy some cooking kitchen foil,he was back home now watching the Jeremy Vine show listening to them talking away about Brexit stating will this country or won't it join up with the E.U concerning Brexit on the 31st october 2019,he wasn't really interested in the brexit debate which he couldn't really avoid for it had been showing on the tv daily for the last nearly 3 years,he just didn't understand it at all,the only thing he thought that it would be probably better if Britain joined with the E.U more than leaving for he believed unity was strenght, oh well he thought as the programme finished,picking up the remote control turning the channel over to ITV to the This Morning programme,oh well he thought concerning Brexit, what is to be will be.

It was not his concern,for he knew exactly where his concerns laid,which was to somehow get all the books he had written advertised,he had written over 45 small books of Knowledge each one averaging 80-100 pages he had also written and completed 2 adventure novels he had put onto the amazon kindle system as paperback and e.books.

Stephen also had many art works he had created which he would in time be putting onto canvas then into selected frames so then maybe in the later oncoming future days he would be able to show them off in some art galleries.

Strangely though he had already met up with a person who had become friendly with him this passing summer who was an artist his name was junior,who had already created some beautiful drawings,junior also had an art exhibition happening on the 6th october it was just a few days ago last sunday infact in an area called Homerton in the borough of Hackney where stephen use to live in the early 1990's up until 2011.

He met junior through another new friend he had met early this year while working summer 2019 as a steward for a security company,this person's name was jaycee he was a security officer working for the same company.

Stephen was allocated one day to work in a area called Leyton in east london at a Hockey and Tennis stadium as a steward,it's there he met jaycee,they worked a few shifts together throughout the summer season,jaycee making mention to him on one of their shifts he was going to the Bristol carnival in a few weeks time,stephen then telling him he had two brothers living in bristol city and he was also going to the carnival,that day they agreed with each other to travel together to the carnival in the weeks ahead jaycee also telling him he had a friend who was to be going to the carnival with him whose name was junior,this was how stephen who was known as birdy met up with junior the day before the bristol carnival 2019 at the london victoria coach station.

That day birdy was also to be meeting up with an old friend of his named eden at the same time at the coach station for 9pm.

Birdy eden jaycee and junior all met at the coach station birdy turning up totally drunk,if it weren't for eden and jaycee birdy would not of been able to board the coach,eden and jaycee speaking some words of wisdom into the coach drivers ears performming their miracles.

Jaycee and junior didn't know eden and junior didn't know birdy at that time and moment at the coach station before boarding the coach.

CHAPTER
2   OCCUPIED

The natural time clock was surely ticking away time was certainly on the move it was now countdown to 2020 the ending of a second decade since the new millennium,still Stephen's pockets were on the very low in fact he was broke totally skint he had been only doing part time work with the security company since losing his driving licence last summer for accumulating speeding points in the process losing his driving job working as a delivery driver for a logistic company for over 2 years he had been living now for 2 years in this private one bedroom flat while being in a relationship with a black British lady whose name was sarina he had hardly spent time at his own place for he was now mostly at her home in finchley north london she was a few years younger than hims being in her mid-thirties with two children they had been together now 2 years, she had a 18 years old daughter and a 11 years son,Stephen's son Jaydon who was 12 years old from his ex-partner abina would spend time with him at Sarina's playing and having fun with maalik playing football outside by the front door of the flat or out in the nearby park when ever stephen and sarina took out door walks to the park in the area.

He was at sarina's home yesterday leaving there late last night going back to his flat on his own there he rested on his bed on this early friday afternoon watching the challenge programme on his tv of another episode of the The Chase

Nathaniel.s. Bird

while smoking a roll up.

CHAPTER
3   BROTHER'S

Just over 120 miles away in bristol city stephen's two other brother's alex and mark were also chilling mark stephen's younger brother who had just celebrated his 39th birthday up in london with stephen and their sister christine had only just left london the sunday past having spent 3 weeks up in london with stephen and christine he was now in his bedroom in his brother alex's two bedroom flat where he had been living with his brother the past few years his prison years now left behind him after serving his sentence in High Down london prison which ended in 2014 spending his last few months sharing a cell with his cousin leroy douglas who was only on the phone talking to stephen for a few minutes yesterday from his cell in the Bristol prison where he had been transferred to in 2018 he was still incasarated still stuck in the prison system 14 years had passed yet he still found himself behind prison getting rejected every time he was up for patrol board hoping to win his parole then happily leave the prison gates behind feeling free now to go home but no this just didn't happen spending now his 38th birthday in the pen.

The time was now 12.51pm warmly friday afternoon the weather in bristol was just like the weather in grey skies with damp wet concrete roads the hot summer season of the record breaking weather had completely vanished bringing in the autumn rains as the climate had quickly plummeted it was the time for bringing out the umbrella's with hood jackets or the wearing of woolly hats it wasn't cold enough as yet for the scarf with gloves.

Inside alex's flat in the easton area of bristol the heating was switched to on the whole of his two bedroom flat was comfortably warm, mark laid there on his double bed clothed in his black tracksuit bottoms with his white vest on watching the tv in his room while alex was upstairs on the next floor of the apartment of the building in a neighbours flat a dreadlock elder whose name was errol,alex had been living at this apartment 10 years now while errol had been there nearly 9 year both knew each other before moving into this apartment building errol originally coming from london city to bristol in the earlier years being born in jamaica, alex had only just a few minutes ago knocked on errol's flat door he was now sitting on the leather sofa in his living room waiting for him to get fully dressed for they both intended to go out to the allotment to gather in some fresh vegetables errol had been growing.

CHAPTER 4   TIMES

The money tap seem to be slowly turning itself towards off than getting more and more turned on ,it certainly wasn't flowing for those people of the working class it just seem to be like drips and drabs dropping down from out of it no more floods neither flows not eve streams just drips it seem like times were growing harder instead of easier for those who were fortunate those who were not born into wealth with riches the challenges of life was surely on the war had long ago begun the battle for cash the casualties were on the increase the damage was being done the inflicted were getting more inflicted with financial injuries the poorer people were hurting the days which the ticking of time seem to be bringing around were difficult days filled up with troubles filled with hardness something just was not right for it if were then the working class would of been gladly progressing even if slowly things just weren't correct, why were so many shops on the high streets closing all over the country many large major stores which had once been greatly established in the country for many decades now ended up shutting their shop doors for the final time doing business no more even business with companies shutting close their doors some people now blaming shopping on line on the internet for some of the shop closure's then to add more injury on the injured those who found themselves on the unemployment benefit long line were now finding themselves placed onto a brand-new benefit system ,no more old time jobseekers allowance which they had grown use to but they knew benefit system which was called universal credit was now newly functioning which many who were now on it was far from pleased believing to themselves the old system worked much better the once a fortnight government money they use to receive had now changed to once a month which meant they had to be more careful in how they managed and spent the little amounts of money they received for if they fell short long before the month was completed they knew they would be finding themselves in distress they would have no option but to go to the food voucher stores to collect for themselves free food things were changing rapidly from better to worse it seemed for the working class with those stuck on the benefit system especially for those who loved to smoke a little tobacco of cigarettes also having for themselves a cheap drink for now in those days with times all the small cheap packets of tobacco had been gotten rid of which were not expensive to buy when they use to be on sale the average packet then was around £3 now in these days the cheap packets of tobacco in the corner shops with supermarkets were no less than £10 while some of the cheap strong lagers in single tin cans had doubled in their prices what was going on Birdy use to think to himself because he loved a little smoke and a drink this is crazy it's really getting more harder for mr and mrs Poor he often though while he moved through the times of these passing days trying to keeping focused on his own personal plans he didn't wish to see himself sinking in these times financially even though he already was, he was out of position not in position while trying to somehow get himself into a secured position, yes he thought to himself these are definitely challenging times but also knowing to himself these past 13 months since losing his driving licence with his delivery job it was like a blessing in disguise because it now gave him more free time to download the kindle app then upload all his books he had written one book at a time onto the amazon kindle system while struggling on forward doing part time work it was like he could see signs with warnings up ahead in the oncoming nearing distance of times and they were not good signs definitely not for all those belonging to the working class every single he was doing right now was toward preparing for this mysterious future which laid ahead of the whole of mankind preparing creating designing his own personal money making machine which he had already done he had already put his created invention together having screwed in the last few secured screws with bolts tightening them up tightly then placing it on the amazon kindle system the art work would be the next thing for him to tighten up securely securing before joining up on some future art exhibition maybe with junior introducing his arts to the art world.

Stephen was on a mission but it was a patient mission which he knew from the very start from the mid 1990's when he started the first of his first written invention now he knew new skills were needed this was to get himself known he had to somehow advertise himself for he knew although he had written so many books no one knew who he was neither did they know his author's name he know knew he was soon to be starting this knew challenge of getting his name out there in the industry so then he would be able to fortunately see his books selling.

The challenging games of life was still on he already knew he was a born competitor joined in with every single man with woman on this planet in this world all competing one against the other all who disbelieved who didn't take the games seriously believing they were not in a race would be certainly fooling themselves for the race they were in including every other living human was called the human race.

CHAPTER 5
THE MONEY LADDER

Right there right in the midst of the whole of mankind the fine spectacular money ladder stood looking expensive dear and very fantastic it had been mysteriously placed right there in front of the faces of all the children of men it was placed right there on earth for a special purpose a specific reason it's rungs rose up pass the white fluffy spongey floating drifting white clouds right up through the heavenly blue skies the high top precious rungs could not be spotted neither seen by a single human eye it was placed in front of billions of pairs of human eyes in front of the rich and the poor the wise and the foolish the crafty with the cunning the honest with dis-honest.

Why was it placed there in this human race why was it created then placed right there on earth with it's very expensive fine precious steps which carried all the cash money of this gigantic planet, those who were fortunate to step on its wealthy healthy rungs slowly but surely rose up into riches they would certainly be leaving the petty cash right behind them in times past while gathering in collecting receiving all the desires of their hearts with wishful dreams knowing to themselves the higher up you were fortunate to climb then the more all things became possible each positive sure step up they took was more the cash money added up then started to multiply passing all those small little thousands of pounds moving on swiftly pass the tens of thousands those who were wise intelligent shrewd also smart would find themselves in time reeling it in, collecting it while counting up the money in its huge stacks with piles while their faces carried happy smiles because it was all clean honest money they were receiving in their lives, the money ladder held onto all the money in this material world million's billion's trillion's upon trillion's there was more than enough money up there to share out equally also fairly to every single person in this world on this human planet every single person on earth could if they were clever enough became a millionaire billionaire even trillion ire's it was all down to the heart in their chest with the ways of how they were thinking it was all down to their thought process.

Many there were of the working class who were born without an inheritance starting their poor lives living in empty days short in their money pockets their wallets with purses always holding small change always close to empty these were the unfortunate the under-privilege the poorer people of the lands living all of this world in all continents in every country every city town with villages the colour of their skin didn't come into the equation they were just people men women boys girls real people poor people all a part of this daily modern moving generation born living while growing up in poor suburbs living in housing estates ghetto slums shanti towns depraving area's all over the world in Africa the Caribbean islands America South America Asia China Japan in all nations many getting not a single head start in this real life their parent not given not fortunate to get that lucky break in their life time to establish wisely setting up themselves so they may be able to safely prepare a positive way forward for their children growing up daily in their lives so there they dwelt daily living in a rich material world filled with durable riches while they all greatly lacked it's treasure's.

Temptations laid on every single bend with corners in a lot of these working class growing children lives for there was so much material fine quality substances glowing glittering finely shinning showing of its decorative beauties out there in the high street shops with shopping malls very expensive manmade inventions in the car sales showrooms with jewellery shops digital stores clothes with sports shops the material world they lived in sharing with the super-rich wealthy with all those who were famous it was flooded filled up to the brim with fantastic fabulous treasures of all sorts shapes with kinds but every single item carried a price tag nothing was free not even the food which was to be daily consumed eaten from off their plates many of the young growing teenagers who's pockets were always on the low with those of early adulthood who had no inheritance placed into their hands knew they were a million pounds away from a million pounds knowing their feet were not on the money ladder neither were their parent's not even on the very first rung which started at a flimsy grand their feet's stood in poverty,for it was in the poverty pits they know realised they had been living all their young lives,they also knew there was plenty of money to be made with many lovely splendid items to be bought which were waiting for them out there in the human society,but many didn't know the short honest route in coming into vast amounts of wealthy riches with material treats,no they just didn't know the way how to climb up the rungs of that precious money ladder neither did many of their parents even their grandparents who had already lived their past lives and were now buried being no more having lived out their days without the abundance of riches,their option were only to join onto the long hard toiling labouring tasks of holding down small time jobs earning a small weekly monthly salary giving,their time of day submitting themselves to their employers bosses managers knowing the progress to riches in this direction was patiently slow while seeing most of their honest earned money going to paying bills loans with debts but also knowing there was nothing they could do about this.

There were other children of the working class family who found other ways after leaving their schooling vicinities with little or no education into trying to come into some fast easy cash trying their best by any means in getting their feet's firmly onto the money ladder,coming up with cunning scheming devices deceptive dishonest behaviours trying to find ways of robbing stealing cheating swindling lying to get their filthy dirty hands with feet's onto the money ladder they were now know to be called the children of vanity who had lost their human place with mental spot now carrying around with them that strange mental mark in their minds the mark of confusion always going the wrong way about in how to achieve their earnings not even realising their feet's will never step properly onto the rungs of the expensive ladder for as soon as they stepped onto it they found themselves forever slipping back off it their cash money will never progressively prosper in time but does always go back down on the decline looking dull without a shine for only honest feet's are found upon the money ladder steps only good wise sensible intelligent shrewd smart feet's it's those type of feet's which will find themselves successfully on the higher climb.

The money ladder was specially placed in the midst of mankind among the children of men to test their integrity to divide the honest from the dishonest,seeing who were they who intended to play the games of life fairly but greater was the temptations on the poor people's side who out of the poor would trade their honesty for deceitful unjust riches who would stay poor and honest also who could rise up into riches with their honesty intacted,those who were born into riches well strongly established in the lands owing lands properties business those who firmly held onto the strong cash solid money being handed down a healthy inheritance whose financial figures in their banks accounts were fat their feet's were already on this treasure ladder they were fortunate to be born on it and they intended to stay on it for they knew with money comes power also position their children having grown up seeing their families already set in a perfect position

in society never being in the position where they are dispar-
ately in wants with needs money certainly was the answer to
the solution of their problems it was the antidote for the rich
with the poor people needed but fell short of knowing how to
greatly achieve it the growing children of the rich and famous
knew they had a great exciting future laid up in store for them
they knew whatever hearts desires they had in mind would
and will be achieved their future days were solid secure finely
set if they behaved those who were rich and safely living on
the money ladder had very little material worries their only
worries were in not losing their wealthy positions while making sure their little growing children grew up wise enough
learning to look after the family treasure and to also add on to
it they were at a great advantage in the challenging games of
human life.

CHAPTER 6 AT HOME

Stephen sat there that friday afternoon in his one bedroom
private flat in his living room on his own relaxing with his
mind filled up with honest thoughts and ambitions plans he
knew he was in the class of the unfortunate one's having being
all of his life he was also fully aware of the money ladder
placed right there in front of the whole of mankind he was also
hungry and thirsty for riches so he too could taste the finer
things in life he also had been living with empty pockets all
his life yes he knew his passed teenage years up to the age of
22years old he was walking the sly slippery dodgier roads of
crime being involved in criminal activities which had caused
him to find himself spending many a time in the prison system
locked away behind steel doors and iron bars all for the sake
of trying to earn for himself some dirty cash, tasting the prison
life several times never enjoying its taste, thinking it tasted
terrible very awful, the wasting of precious ticking time making up his mind while being locked away behind prison cell
doors that he didn't wish to be coming back in here no more
when the time come for him to be released set free regaining
back his priceless liberty arriving reaching the crossroads in
life of decision and choosing the decision of ridding himself of
crooked crimes learning now to walk the straight honest long
patient pathway to riches also to learn to be a honest con-
tender in the games of life all this was embedded in the mind
of Stephen knowing now that if he was to climb the money
ladder it had to be climbing it one fair honest step at a time..

He had been creating his own work of art with patience throughout the moments of moving time, now here he sat alone in his chair in his living room inside f his flat in the time jump nearly 3 decade on and he was still living in the midst of poverty near to broke doing part time jobs here and there with not a single foot on the first rung of the money ladder he already knew deep in himself that patience meant patience but the waiting game surely was not easy he had come to realise when you are living through empty desolate days weeks with months which turns into years then decades he could also see and clearly understand why it was so easy for those people belonging to the working class to easily give up then take the cunning crafty criminal ways of crimes for destruction was in the poverty, poverty has no mercy he could see for it stripes bare laying waste ruins then destroys people with their characters bringing them down to the values of that which is less than a price of a piece of bread bringing them to nothing.

He got up from where he was sitting walked just a few feet infront of him to the glass coffee table picked up his mobile started tapping on a few numbers standing there on his red gold and green coloured rug which was on top of his laminated floored living room in his black Nike tracksuit bottoms with white t-shirt on then walked those few steps back taking his seat once again while listening to the ringing tone in his ear waiting for the call to be answered,

a voice came over the phone saying

hi dad how are you

I'm fine ashley how are you doing there in Port Talbot

Stephen hadn't spoken to his older son for a few weeks knowing ashley was a independent 30 years lad always working,

are you still working in the barber shop son

yes dad I'm there right now ,how are you ?

i'm fine son although things could be better still

how's my brother jaydon and myles

they are okay I will bring them down to visit you hopefully before the years is out

he stayed on the phone talking to ashley for another 10 minutes before ashley told his dad he had to go back to work

alright son speak soon ok

ok dad ashley said before his voice disappeared and the mobile phone went silent.

stephen pressed a few more digits on his mobile phone then waited for an answer

hi alright stephen what's up,hi babes you ok he replied,it was his partner on the phone,what are you doing today ? sarina asked

I got no plans babe,

well why don't you come back to my place

okay he replied,I will get the bus up to yours in a hour or so

okay she answered,I will see you when you come

okay I will see you soon,stephen said before disconnecting himself from his mobile phone.

CHAPTER 7
CRAZY TIMES

Every day pubs were closing shutting their front doors for the last time not opening them anymore,more shops on the high streets were closing their doors for good also, zero contracts was now the new thing many business with employment companies were starting to introduce to their employees the times in the UK were changing, knife crimes was on the rise many a young teenager in london city were losing their young lives it was now beginning to become a weekly thing another teenager has been stabbed to death another parent grieving losing a brother or a sister a relative has lost a cousin a uncle and aunt has lost a young nephew or niece these stabbing yearly seemed to be continuing year after year these last few year mostly young black youths stabbing one another to death the grown adults of all race could not see any sense in this neither could Stephen in his eyes they were all just young teenagers slowly blossoming in life not yet fully grown having no life experience but willing to pick up a shank blade then stick it into somebody, Stephen often thought to himself they were completely blind youths not thinking about their future but living for the hyped up here and now they must believe in themselves there is no future this is why they are utterly showing they don't give a damn neither do they care right well they were completely wrong because there always will be a future and they will be a part of it whether they like it or not, maybe their future maybe one which is very dim finding themselves now locked up in societies prisons system because their past have caught up with them in an entirely different way in an emotional mental way for now their young developing minds just can't handle the inner guilt which seem to be now daily tormenting their minds now realising they have stepped in way to deep into the wrong activities completely disrespecting this life knowing personally to themselves they are now a murderer now not liking neither loving their image which now confronts then every time they look in the mirror.

Things seem to be more out of control also uncertain in these days with times more than positive and sure people more out of control than fully in control of themselves,mental health was on the rise so to was depression in many of the peoples minds in the big cities peace and love could only be easily spotted and found in the small towns with villages there also trust among the neighbours could be found, there seem to be more love among one another in the neighbouring country towns with villages while there seem to be a fire burning brightly in the hearts with minds of those dwelling in the large busy cities.

A change needed to come needed to appear sooner much more than later,eitherwise many more young teenagers blood would be spilt on the streets of London because of knife crime with other cities in the UK,real support the parent's of those who lost their children were crying also calling out for not wishing for anymore parent's to go through the empty feelings of lost which they were now going through also experiencing real pain real loss of a real young member of their family,they were very upset also angry their hearts now filled to the brim of sorrowful bitterness,there was certainly troubles to be seen on every bend with corners ghetto living was not a good living from what was to be shown weekly on the tv news programmes it was far away from pleasant.

The trust had been removed from the hearts of many

people who lived in london city,it was now the days of learning to fully trust your ownself with your own instinct-s,a stranger was to be looked on as a total stranger,if people didn't know you then they would show it by completely ig-noring showing no interest what so ever,their ways may seem completely ignorant to the real strangers who had just arrived into this city with a friendly go lucky attitude but this person would soon quickly realise this wasn't always a warm friendly place to be unless you were with warm friendly people who knew exactly who you were,this was just the self-protect-ing mechanism shield the experience person who grew up or spent a long time in this city operated,shielding while pro-tecting themselves from oncoming dangers.

Three quarters of the year 2019 had already been spent just 2 months existed after october had completely run its course everyone wants also wishes to be celebrating new year's eve while welcoming in another brand-new year of 2020 not desiring to be another victim of the year 2019.

Pubs were still being closed shut down daily also weekly while shops closed its doors for good here and there all over the UK,when was the doors closing of pubs shops with business going to stop shutting,not one single person knew the answer to this puzzling question.

CHAPTER 8
OUR WORLD

What a wonderful world we all live

which spins around and around and around

it doesn't stop spinning around while daily

we all walk it's ancient earthly worldly grounds.

   Though there are many people

   who don't understand this precious gift of life

   they have been freely given which is priceless

   which doesn't cost a single price

   they resort to deadly weapons

   picking up destructive weapons like guns with knives.

The youths with teenagers

are way too young to fully appreciate

also understand how precious their lives are

they need to swiftly wake up also be counted

they really need to realize who they are.

   Our plant which stretches itself out

   for miles upon miles

   it stretches itself out for thousands of miles

   from one end of this earth

right over to its other immortal side.

didn't you know neither did you realise

Our world is filled with wonders

while around and around our world does spin

while at times we all witness with surprise

it's lightening's with noisy rumbling thunders

everyone of us are competitors in this world

the rich with the poor the foolish with the wise

you are looking at me strange through your seeing eyes

I think to myself you don't even know who I am

you don't even consider neither realise.

Remember everyone has hearts desires

we all have wishful wonderful dreams

I do know nothing is impossible

while you are joined onto this superior

human team.

So on and on time does move while ticking

silently telling you the race has to be run

be intelligent smart shrewd also clever

make sure you are gathering some decent

honest money lump sum.

Don't allow yourself to follow

the foolishness of folly

certainly you are not counted as wise if you do

I wish you the best of luck

in the selections of choices

which are now confronting you.

Every single one of us are on a treasure hunt

we all want to successfully achieve

me you with everybody

including the muggers robbers

with cunning crooked thieves

the battle for cash has long ago started

who are they who will be walking away

packed stacked with a big bag filled up with clean cash

I do know you would love to

also know you love the sound of that.

Today is just another day

another brand-new twenty four hours given to you also me

it's filled up with wonderful wonders

it's filled with hidden secret beautiful mysteries.

I have hit the one million pound figure mark

my bank account is loaded with fine clean cash

the woman I love I have even caught

then securely catch

then in the morning I wake up

realising it was all just a dream.

Once again it's back to being Mr Poor man

it's the life I daily seem to be living

I know if I was Mr Wealthy or maybe Mr Rich

I would be happily dispersing

while willingly always handing out also giving

Walking the roads with streets
while my pockets are greatly lacking
it's not pleasant to my living beating heart
there are so many wonderful things
beautiful substances
my eyes are constantly noticing while spotting
but I do know I can't afford to freely buy.

> They say life is what you make of it
> but it's extremely hard
> making something out of nothing
> when you are joined onto
> the working class daily doing hard labours
> which always seem to count for nothing.

You had better swiftly wake up to realise
you too are also involved
in the human challenging games
it's been going on
for thousands upon thousands of years
right up to these present modern days with ages.

> It shall continue on way passed this oncoming future
> way up into the new futuristic times
> which have not yet come
> human life will always be firmly established
> on this planet inside of this world
> it will never ever be extinguished
> over then finally done.

Never ever forget your secret mysterious friend

who have been with you

from the time of your given birth

your personal mystical mystic friend

is a natural blessing

please do not cover its powers all over with a dark curse.

   Because it's a wonderful world we all live in

   sharing it with each other every single moving day

   I do hope you are counting blessings after blessings

   in every single beautiful wonderful

   mysterious marvellous way

Didn't you not know life is filled with beautiful colours

it's filled with the beautiful colours of life

you don't need to make it

difficult horrendous neither very hard

you are suppose to make it become sweet

pleasant pleasing always nice.

   Please don't get things twisted

   neither mixed up totally the wrong way around

   upside down

   for if this is the cause with case

   you will not be the big bread winner

   travelling through the big cities

   it's small country towns.

This life is created for all of us

who are here today living

for this is a living life

we are here to live life the best we can

we are all here to be fully living only once not twice.

So always learn to put your best foot forward

as you are walking along through

the moving times of days

as the time clock continues to keep ticking forward

I do hope durable treasure's appear soon

along your pathway.

The waiting game is not easy

especially if patience is one thing you don't have

at times in this life you have got to stop and think

you can't be always running all around

acting crazy and mad.

Just continue to remember

it's a beautiful wonderful life we are given

it's beauties reaches right up into

the blue heavenly skies

which stands up tremendously high

it's filled with fantastic natural creations

also filled up with wonderful people

just like you and even I.

◆ ◆ ◆

CHAPTER 9
TRAVELLING ALONG

The orange digital letters inside of the bus shelters stop was showing all those waiting for the 102 bus to Finchley was due in one minute there were a few people standing there waiting when the bus arrived,the front door to the red double decker bus opened it's front door with all it's side double doors allowing it's passengers on the inside of the bus to use its double side doors to step off the bus while those who waited outside the bus started to climb aboard using the TFL transport for London blue and white oyster card or their bus passes some passengers tapped the digital device beside the bus driver with their bank cards if they didn't have a oyster card or used their mobile phone with the buses fair app they had downloaded onto their mobile phones for all the London transport buses didn't use cash to board their buses for the cash system was now a thing of the past.

Stephen stepped on the bus tapped his oyster card on the digital device then made his way towards the stairway up the steps to the top deck of the bus while realising on the walk there the downstairs deck was nearly full,most of it's seats were taken as he got to the top deck he had a choice of a few seats for it wasn't too busy on this deck,he walked straight to the back of the bus to its back seat seeing they were empty,taking himself a seat on the far left right next to the window,so he could look out through,getting a good look out through it,getting a view of whatever whenever he wished,he made himself comfortable while the bus started out on its journey slowly leaving edmonton green behind moving on through the city traffic.

Stephen made himself comfortable sitting there at the back dressed in black jean with his black waist length leather jacket on with his black cap on his head while he relaxed his feet in his black Nike trainers his beard covered the side of his face neatly but slightly shaved while he looked ahead of him at the back of the heads of the few passengers sitting in the seats in front of him,right at the front of the bus he could see above the window a digital information board showing the name of the next bus stop while the device spoke the name of the stop then showed what time in the day it was.

After several stops on the bus journey the bus stopped a short time at a bus stop as Stephen was looking out of the back left side window he looked down towards the bus stop,he could see a load of school children boys with girls around the age of 12 and 13 years old boarding the bus in their school uniforms all going up the stairs to the top deck filling up the back seats of the bus all talking noisily and loudly to one another,as they were speaking to one another Stephen just sat there in his seat positioned watching them talking while at times looking out of the window as the bus continued on its journey forwards.

It was another 15 minutes before all the school children got off,before he got to the bus stop he needed to get off he pressed the buzzer alerting the driver then walked down from the top deck down the stairs to the centre double doors waiting behind a few passengers who were also waiting to get off,the bus slowed down then stopped,the area he was now in was called Finchley in the North of London he stepped off the bus as the doors opened up then took the few minutes walk to the apartment building where Sarina his partner lived.

CHAPTER 10
MONEY MAKES OUR WORLD GO AROUND

Didn't you not know money makes

our world go around?

the American dollars with the English pounds

the battle for cash it's far away from over and done

the roars with cries of the poor voices

are not low but high

the children of the poor

don't just want but they also need

naturally everybody wishes to progress also succeed

but when your family is always living on the bread line

when things seem always bleak

with nothing guaranteed.

We as their parents can't give up neither give in

don't lose focus

for we are constantly out to achieve

while we daily walk through

this earthly worldly mysterious time

we are determined to bring poverty

crashing right down upon its knees.

I am on the journey of life

I am on a mysterious mystical marvellous mission

when a person is stripped bare

of fine luxurious treasure's

it will feel like they are doing

a life sentence in a top security prison.

To rise up from out of poverty

to be glorious in winning the battle for cash

holding onto my shield of knowledge

with my sword of wisdom

I will shatter dismantle

also destroy then completely utterly smash.

I will not allow the power of money

to turn my character into a criminal

neither a cunning crooked thief

the ways of wrongs with injustice

from my essence it will always have to flee.

Birdy the black guy from Port Talbot South Wales

he is on a money mission

book one with book two

are already published with book three

they are all written

for a purpose with a positive reason.

Many more books he have written

in E.Book with paper back form

google the name of this author

you will see his book titles go on and on.

So please remember clearly do not forget this

those who are determined shall succeed

in time you will not find them caught up

in the trailing behind losing pack

their hands shall be holding

onto the goblet of victory.

The time clock will always be ticking forward

passing new days weeks with months also years

so learn to hold on fast to that thing called patience

then in time it will bring your dreams

with desires right near.

Actions speaks for wealth remember

positive actions we wish to see

for with positive movements

progress will spring up exposing prosperity.

◆ ◆ ◆

CHAPTER 11
SARINA

As Stephen entered into the 3 bedroom apartment closing the door behind him walking through the hallway into the living room finding sarina sitting there on the black leather sofa he walked up to her then gave her a kiss on the side of her cheek,she smiled at him as he took a seat beside her

why don't you take your jacket off and put it on the coat hanger ? she said

looking to her left side at stephen

yeah I will now he said resting back into the sofa

her young son was in his bedroom playing his computer games her daughter wasn't at home but still at her college

before stephen had come into the home sarina was watching the tv which she went back to watching

after a few minutes stephen put his jacket on the coat hanger in the hallway then told her he was going into the bedroom where there was a hard drive monitor with a keyboard so he could continue on the only book he had left to write finish and complete,he sat down on a small office type looking chair near the window which was placed right next the computer system slightly bent himself down switched on the power button getting himself ready to bring up the file he needed to continue on with his project ,his phone in his jeans front pocket started to ring,he pulled it out looked at it,the caller was his older sister lucy who lived in Port Talbot, he answered the call sat back while looking towards his left at the bedroom window covered over with a white netted cur- tain dropping itself down onto the window sill in-between the thick blue opened curtains

Hi sister how are you?

hello stephen his sisters voice said down the phone,then she started explaining to him there was going to be a reggae night in the town on November 5th Bonfire night at Jimmy's Bar

mm sounds interesting,stephen told her,then said he would get back to her because there were still a few weeks to go be- fore the event,

the last time he had seen lucy was a few months ago when he went down to Wales for the weekend to visit her and his other older sister jean

After he had finished talking with his sister he placed the mo- bile phone on the window sill just beside him then started to focus once again working on his writing project.

CHAPTER
12　　　　THE
WORLD WE LIVE IN

Billion's of people walk this planet

beneath the yellow sun

below those floating silver twinkling stars

men women boys girls

belonging to our superior human race.

　Back White Chinese Indian

　different colours with different shades of skin

　belonging to this 21st century's modern generation

　daily they are all living out their lives

　Kings with Queens's princes with princess's

　presidents with prime ministers

　tramps beggars vagrants living a shabby tattered life

　a lot of them seem somewhat lost

　in the days derisions with confusion's.

People of different mentalities

people with different chains of thoughts

people living a high life feeling free

while you have those who are completely caught.

    People living in beautiful palaces high wall castles

    standing there looking fabulous

    spectacular very grand

    butler's standing at the entry doors

    keeping up their daily duties with their daily plans.

Some living in lovely manors

surrounded by acres of healthy looking green lands

others in modern mansions with large swimming pools

I do hope you understand.

it's back to the money topic

while we are daily living in this land.

    People sleeping at night in the dark park

    some inside of sleeping bags

    sleeping outside by shop windows

    sleeping outside in the elements

    while the rain falls

    while the snow falls while the windy breeze

    constantly howls and blows.

All types of people

coming from different background

still we all are people

none of us are aliens.

    Alcoholics drug addicts

    prostitutes the ladies of the nights

    crack cocaine heroin class a drugs

always right in front of their seeing sights.

Silver foil injection syringes

sharp razor blades

sniffing snorting smoking chasing

drugs they want constantly

flowing through their brains with veins

the life some people choose to live

can seem crazy also very insane.

Small sentences long stretches life sentences too

daily waking up in the prison system

being watched constantly by the prison screw's

your freedom has been taken away from you

there is nothing at all about it you can now do.

There are always choices with options

for you to select pick also choose

whether you be rich or poor

standing here in life inside of your shoes.

The poor can make riches

the rich can get even richer if they wish

in this life nothing is impossible

so please now make that special wish

and don't resist

Those who are foolish walk the pathways of destruction

they are very cruel to their own selves

very selfish in their behaviour's

their feet's walk further down into earthly worldly hell.

They grow weaker they do not grow stronger

as ticking time ticks on forward into life

losing their health strength

with youthful beauties

in time they look shameful unpleasant

very far from looking fine not looking nice.

Billion's upon billions of peoples

walking through this life day and night

the caring with the discrete very careful

mixed in with the heartless who have no real plight.

We have people living in dessert lands

deep in the baron wilderness

riding on the backs of camels

some nomads with sandals on their feet's

while they patiently are making

their striding steps

Other's living in the jungles

surrounded by man-eating animals of all kinds

lions leopards jaguars panthers

alligators with long sharpened teeth's

crocodiles which never smiles.

Many eskimos in their igloos

in the white cold lands filled with ice and snow

wearing thick furred skinned garments

they have no choice

for they have to combat fighting the freezing cold..

We all live in a different part of this wonderful world
which is filled up with buried hidden treasures
gold silver ruby's diamonds with precious pearls.
   We have to earn a living
    knowing to ourselves we must not go out and steal
    fishermen drawing back their fishing nets
    loaded with all kinds of fishes
    so people can buy them up
    for their dinner or evening meals.
The farmer milking his cow's
while daily sowing his vegetable crops
he is hoping for a fine healthy harvest
wanting to be soon trading
 good quality healthy food to all the shops.
We who are without a job
must swiftly find for ourselves a labour
a person must have something positive to do
weekly bringing home a pay wage income
while keeping the troubles of crime far away from you.
Doctors nurses midwives surgeons
the hospital wards are busy
from day right up until late into the nights
accident and emergency intensive care
ambulances flashing their blue siren lights.
   Police officers with firemen
   they all have their jobs to do

catching crooks with criminals

putting out fires while coming to your rescue.

There are all types of jobs out there

waiting for you to step into

don't turn yourselves into drug addicts thugs criminals

lost in this worldly life now

taking up the wrong mental view.

Electricians carpenters bricklayers plumbers

all working together on the construction sites

buildings are needed to be built up strongly

of all size shapes forms with designs.

It's a material manmade world we all live in

remember it's their hands with their working tools

which have built this material manmade world

a world filled with man made laws with orders

which we all daily serve

no one wants to get arrested taken away in handcuffs

for it's not what honest people deserve.

Cities cover the whole lands filled with buildings

built by the men and women of mankind

you can not live inside of any of them

without money

so please now show me your intentions

with future plans.

We already know the roads of life

can be rough and very rocky

for those people of the poor working class

it's a very serious challenge for most of them

climbing up the money ladder is a very difficult task.

CHAPTER 13
WHERE HAS THE
LOVE GONE

The power of love seem to be fading swiftly

in the hearts of the people

in this rising new modern generation

they seem to be forgetting

their origin the natural essence

they had been created with

shunning the powers of love

rejecting it ignoring it

while forsaking it for hates abominations.

    Superficial people now

     seem to walk this earthly worldly ground

      their appear looking normal fashionably fine

      but when you really check them out

       you would find there is no real life's knowledge

      inside of them

    they were all just simply followers

    like sheeps walking on side by side

walking straight towards

the direction on the slaughter house

not one not even a single one

had the qualities of a leader

the foolishness of folly filled up their mouths.

Under minding while under-estimating

this is what they would be doing all day long

no mercy was to be inside of their hearts

cursing with swearing

to them this was their sweet songs.

It seemed like they had long forgotten

the time of their day of birth

even why they were created to live a life on earth

no mercy shall be shown to that soul with spirit

when their day of death comes around

when their body is sent back into the dirt

beneath this eternal earthly ground.

Mocking scorning cursing swearing

vile words are always to be found on their tongues

they have no appreciation no value

for this precious priceless life

the real genuine ways of life they daily shun.

Hatred they prefer instead of love

folly instead of wisdom

the understandable words of knowledge

their ears just don't wish to hear neither listen

very disrespectful people

some very old even middle aged

beneath our shinning blazing sun.

Love covers all sins

but their folly is daily being exposed

they wish to see the righteous people

daily carry a burden a heavy load.

Materialistic minds

not really realising this life is only just for a time

they do not wish to wake up and be counted

while they daily dwell here amongst mankind.

A time will come when it will be too late to be sorry

I can see they will be begging on their bending knees

really pleading for some mercy with a bit of sympathy

which they have never shown to you neither to me.

Not a bit of love is to be found in their hearts

it's filled with hatred

covered all over in bitterness

daily they walk these earthly worldly grounds

thinking while foolishly believing

they are the best.

Completely lost in life's confusion's

there is no point even trying to show them the way

they will never listen neither will they learn

until their hairy head of hairs

have passed the colour grey.

The hater's of love

the lovers of negativity

I just swiftly walk on pass them

because they are of no use to me.

What are you going to do?

which way are you going to choose

the peaceful pleasant ways of love

which will enable this person in time to win and not lose.

It's love which creates peace

binding hearts together with hearts

forming unity among the people

it doesn't break down destroy spoil separate

causing people to flee away then quickly depart.

◆ ◆ ◆

CHAPTER 14   A LITTLE JOURNEY

Just over 2 weeks had passed on by it was now 26th October stephen was at his flat in edmonton just heading out of his home's front door on his way to pick up his son from his sons grandmothers home, she lived in an area called wood green it was just a one bus ride journey with quit a lot of stops before he arrived at his bus stop on the 144 bus which would take him around 20-25 minutes depending on the traffic.

Just over the last weekend which had passed the time on the time clocks were put back one hour it was now officially the winter season,he closed his front door then started the walk to the bus station dressed in his black leather jacket black jeans with black sports trainer's on with a black woollen hat with black scarf around his neck the weather was 12 degrees, he was surprised to see then sun glowing in the grey cloudy sky even though he could still feel the chill of the cold while he walked onwards to the bus station only a few minutes away from where he lived, his mind went back to the Sunday weekend which had just passed by thinking of when he was working at the Wembley Stadium as a steward for the day doing a 10.30am start until 18.30pm shift, just like today the sun was in the sky that Sunday morning showing it's golden face in the afternoon to as he stood there in his uniform watching the crowds of American football supporters coming to the venue in their thousands to watch NFL American football at the huge stadium, he felt fine at the start of his shift as he stood there with a few other colleagues all surprised to be looking up at the sun shinning at 10.25am that Sunday morning while he puffed away on a tobacco roll up talking to two black British women with another black British male all meeting each other for the first time none knowing each other also all knowing they would all be placed in their working position in 5 minutes time.

It weren't long before he was standing near one of the entry with exist gates guarding it while directing the customer's coming in also wanting to go out of the venue early for whatever reason it's there he stood accompanied by another steward both working together who was a middle aged white english woman, as the time moved along through that Sunday afternoon passing the 2pm hour it was then he started to feel his hands slowly getting colder and colder realising the lights of the sun had faded, the sun was still there somewhere lost behind a sky filled up with slow moving grey clouds,he could now feel the chill of the cold weather as he stood there talking with his working partner saying to her the climate had changed and that today was the first day of winter,I know she said laughing saying you know what I haven't even turned my watched back my time is one hour ahead of everyone as she now started working on her wristwatch..

Now the weather today brought last Sunday's weather to his mind while he was in his bedroom this morning getting dressed looking out of his window seeing the sun out there smiling,I am not taking no chances he thought,it's hats and scarf for me today he told himself.

Now he was sitting on the 144 bus, which he had left the station nearly 20 minutes ago the bus was fairly packed after stopping at many stops collecting passengers on its journey's route he was only a few stops now away from his son's Granma's house.

CHAPTER 15
ON THE MOVE

It was just over 140 miles away in the capitol city of Wales Cardiff city in the Bute town area of Cardiff docks,Bulla was driving out of his area the docks driving out of cardiff city on the A48 motorway he was going to bridgend town which was 19 miles away there he was meeting up with an old friend of his ryan the dread, bulla had been out of prison now 5years enjoying his fifth year of freedom leaving those iron bars steel doors with prison wings and landings behind, ryan the dread had also been released from the prison system around about the same time as bulla being back out in society 5 years enjoying his freedom also but the both of them were still out there in life taking risky chances hustling and trying to make quick money by any means,both had no intentions of holding down a job working on a 9 to 5 or part time labour,they just believed they weren't cut out for this kind of systematically work slaving for bosses managers supervisors even though Bulla's woman kept pleading with him constantly telling him to leave the criminal activities alone and get a job, what examples are you setting for our young growing son she kept telling him who was now aged 7 she also had a young daughter now aged 3 years old so he now had two kids to look after including his woman who couldn't work because she had the two children to take care of,she was wasting her time telling him to get a proper job because he had never ever done a day's work in his life all he knew was to rob steal and sell drugs and it was what he liked also loved plus he knew he had all the free time he needed not having to give 8 hours of his time 5 days or 6 days of the week to any working company.

He drove on down the motorway listening to the music C.D he had slipped into his cars music system while his mobile phone laid there on the passenger seat beside him while he kepted up with the fast moving traffic in the fast lane edging himself closer and closer to Bridgend town as the artist *VYBZ Kartel* was singing his song *Conjugal visit* loudly through the car speakers ,he took another deep pull on the half smoked spliff of skunk weed that smelt strongly in the car ex-haling filling his both lungs with the smoke before blowing it back out from his mouth,his eyes quickly looked towards the glove compartments a smile appeared on his brown skinned face,the thought of money entered into his mind easy money he thought ,driving onward closing in on bridgend town it was another several minutes before he came off the A48 driving on into the town of bridgend shortly arriving outside of the home of ryan the dread,he parked up his car turned the igni-tion off undid his seatbelt picked up his mobile phone from the passenger seat to quickly call the dread letting him know he was parked up outside of his house.

CHAPTER 16
AT SARINA'S

At the same time back in london city stephen was in his woman sarina's home in the bedroom sitting on the chair infront of the monitor working on his novel while sarina was in the living room watching the early evening programme on the tv screen,stephen's son Jaydon was in maalik's bedroom with him playing computer games,stephen had picked jaydon up from his granma's home then took the 144 bus to muswell hill then they took another bus the 102 to Finchley, Jaydon had a rucksack with him when he left his grans which had all the things he needed,his change of clothing with his bed clothes and his gaming tablet,they both walked to the bus stop then took the red double decker bus to sarina's home,sarina's daughter was in her bedroom relaxing.

Writing was just like therapy to stephen it was also his hobby it was like exercising his mind playing around with words exercising his thoughts waking up his imagination keeping himself intouch with his creative nature challenging his creative abilities he sat there tapping away on his black keyboard watching the letters pop up on the monitors screen while creating new chapters to his new novel,birdy the black guy book 3 as the early evening hours passed on,he looked to the left of him through the opened netted curtains he could see the darkness of the evening,he had been writing for over 2 hours,sarina had only come into the bedroom once about a hour ago asking him if he needed anything at the shop downstairs on the high street for she was about to go out to pick up a few groceries,he told her he was okay and didn't need anything, at that time he decided to leave the computer taking his packet of tobacco with rolling papers and his cigarrete lighter,telling her he was going out the back of the flat for a smoke while she was going to the shop,he quickly popped his head into maalik's bedroom to see how the two young boys were doing

You guys alright he said opening the bedroom door seeing jaydon sitting on the edge of maalik's double bed dressed in his Nike red and white tracksuit top with bottoms on with his white's sports sock looking at his dad standing by the door,

yes dad he answered

maalik sat right beside jaydon on his bed holding the games console control in his hand also,dressed in his blue Adidas t-shirt and blue Adidas tracksuit bottom with blue sports socks on

you alright maalik,stephen asked

Yeah I'm good maalik answered as he took his eyes away the game on the tv screen he was playing with jaydon

looking towards his bedroom door at stephen standing there

alright you guy's enjoy your game okay stephen said before he stepped back then closed maalik's bedroom door

sarina was in the hallway putting her black winter jacket with black fluffy furry hood on it on as stephen said to her

I will see you when you get back

okay stephen I won't be long do you need more tobacco rolling papers

oh yeah could you pick up a small blue packet for me

yeah okay I will she said

okay thanks he replied back before he walked on into the

living room to the back of the flat holding his tobacco and papers with lighter all in his left hand the white looking plastic back door right next to the two large white double glazing windows which were fully covered with wide white netted curtains with two opened burgundy curtains attached to it's curtain rail, the tv was on but the rooms light was turned off he walked through across the light brown laminated wooden floor to the door turned the key which was already in the lock of the door opened it then stepped out closing the door instantly behind him.

CHAPTER 17
MAKING PLAN'S

At the other side of the north london in Palmers Green at luis home he was alone this evening talking on his mobile phone to his friend carlo's while he sat in his living room on his sofa feeling well relaxed infront of him on his living room's coffee table you could see a freshly made zoot laying there inside the ashtray with the finished end of one also in there,a plastic lighter was also in the ashtray,he sat there in his white vest with blue jeans on his bare feet slipped into his brown slippers talking away to carlo's while he held his mobile phone in his hand in front of him turned onto louder speaker

yes carlos make sure your on time I will be here waiting for you

luis stated while his eyes looked around his living room from where he sat relaxed looking at the rooms dark brown cabinet in the left corner of the room next to the tv which had framed photos' of his mother on the top of it with pictures of his older brother and sister also in the centre of all the picture frames was a small coloured portuguese flag on a one foot black wooden

yes I will be waiting he continued to say to his friend as he now gazed down looking at the cream coloured carpet which covered the whole of the floor in the living room

alright next saturday it will be then okay,the 2nd of november bruv,noon,midday okay see you then carlos and make sure they are all weighted on point properly okay carlos said before he dis-connected the call from luis.

luis then placed his mobile phone on the coffee table then picked up his zoot of skunk weed out f the ashtray with the plastic lighter putting the spliff joint into his mouth lighting it up then put the lighter on the coffee table while laying back into his sofa smoking his zoot on the 26th october 2019.

CHAPTER 18
DELIVERY SERVICE'S

Back in South Wales now in Port Talbot town ryan the dread was in his car which was parked up next to bulla's car at the aberavon beach front Bulla's was sitting in the passenger front seat next to the dread who had not long finished talking to a person whose name was Curtis who came from the sandfields estate area of the town.

The dread sat there in his car the ignition was turned off,the front lights of his car were turned on his long black thin dreadlocks dropped right the way down passed his broad shoulders falling on to his lap when he stood up straight showing his tall height of 6 foot 34 inches weighting 19 stones his locks fell right down to his waist,it was only 30 minutes earlier Bulla was parked outside the dread's home waiting for the dread in his car moments after phoning the dread he watched the dread open up his front door walked out closing it behind him then walking over to bulla's car

come on then he said standing right in front of bulla's car bulla sitting in his driver seat with his driver's window halfway down looking at the dread standing there in front of him with his dark round face dreadlocks openly showing dropping down his back while some fell passed his shoulders down passed his front waist while he wore a thick pair of dark black glasses were you could see his eyes clearly through its frame

ready or not here we come,he said with a smirk and a little laugh.

he looked at bulla sitting there

curtis is waiting for us

I'm ready to roll bulla said,turning on his ignition waking up his car while watching the dread walk over to his car parked only a few car's down from his home on his street opening the door jumping in then starting up his car.

The person they were going to meet in Port Talbot curtis was originally from Port Talbot being born in neath hospital 5 miles away from the town where most people in the town were born for neath hospital was the nearest hospital in the earlier decades which delivered all new-born babies there was no delivery hospitals for childbirth in port talbot town in the 60's 70's he was Born in 1977 just celebrating his 42nd birthday the month before in september,he met the dread for the first time when he was doing a 2 year prison sentence in the prison system meeting him in the Park prison the end of 2014 when the dread was coming to the end of his sentence the dread was sitting on his single iron bed in his cell all on his lonesome one late october evening his old cell mate had been released a few weeks back so ryan the dread had no cell mate but this didn't bother him,he was independent also had no need for anything he had all the luxuries an inmate needed to get through each day without asking anyone for anything he also enjoyed the freedom of being on his own,he was sitting there on his iron bed watching the cell's tv knowing the evenings association time would soon be starting in about 30 minutes when all cell doors on the landings would be unlocked so all prisoners could leave their cells for one and a half hours to walk the landings or the ground floor play a game on the pool table watch the big screen tv in the tv room or do a bit of socialising with the other inmates,as he sat there he could hear footsteps on the landing which suddenly stopped outside his cell door ryan the dread looked towards his right towards his cell door as he sat there the noise of keys on chains could be heard then a key going into the keyhole of his cell door his cell door opened up wide

in here lad,said the voice of the prison officer,as the prison officer looked in at the dread

meet your new cellmate directing curtis into the cell who was holding his bed pack with white pillowcase which had items inside of the pillowcase like a plastic knife fork and spoon plastic mug toothbrush with a few other small items he walked into the cell fully dressed in prison clothes,before the prison officer slammed the cell door shut behind him.

CHAPTER 19

DELIVERY SERVICES

For the next few weeks the dread and curtis get to know each other better the both got along fine curtis was 5 foot 10 inches chubby built brown hair fellow who had many coloured tattoos covering both his arms you would rarely see him in prison shirts or jumpers and jackets he always wore a prison t-shirt or white vest so he could proudly show off his tattooed arms the 2 year sentence handed to him by the magistrates court was for the possession of class A drugs if he was not on police bail at the time when he was stopped by the police for speeding he would of been given a much shorter lighter sentence because it was only a small amount of cocaine which was found in his possession barely a gramme in weight £60 to £70 in value.

Curtis was on bail at the time waiting to attend the court house in a week before the speeding incident for an assault charge GBH grievous bodily harm instead of the magistrates placing him on remand they gave him bail just two weeks before the speeding offence charge bail with conditions that he stayed out of trouble before he was due back in front of the judge in 3 weeks time,that day he walked out of court with a few of his friends feeling good infact he felt fantastic because he thought he was going to get sent down, that day he was mentally prepared to taste some prison porridge once again,he wasn't a stranger to the prison system having been there several times in the past only on small stretches with a few remands here and there but he definitely wasn't a stranger to the iron bars with steel cell doors of the prison wings with landings.

That same day he got stopped for speeding he was driving his car with two of his mates with him ching in the passenger frontseat foxy sitting in the back of the car, they were just going to Swansea city 9 miles away from Port Talbot just for a spin to pass some time away curtis was smoking a joint of ash while he sped down the dual carriageway of Fabien way reaching speeds of up to 105 mph when he was spotted by a parked up hidden out of sight police vehicle which quickly turned on its blue lights and sirens chasing after him foxie looked behind through the cars back window when he heard the siren's telling curtis the police are coming

curtis quickly lifted his foot of the accelerator peddle dropping his speed quickly below 60 MPH but it was to quick and to late because the police car was already at the side of his car in the slow lane moving at speed pointing signalling for him to pullover and undo his seatbelt,two policemen were already out of their car and by the side of his car yelling at him to get out of his car ching and foxie sat there in their seats quiet while curtis secretively had dropped his joint he was smoking onto the floor by his foot near the gas pedal as he opened his car door then climbed out

what's up officer's,he said nervously

you have been caught speeding one of the policemen said, standing right infront of him

I weren't going that fast curtis tried to explain

105 MPH is not that fast,is that so the second police man

responded

what's that smell the officer who first spoke,standing right by curtis,s driver door asked looking into the car at ching sitting there in the passenger's seat while Foxie sat there watching eyes wide opened at the back of the car

what smell ? curtis answered

the officer pushed his head in through the opened car door,then spotted a half smoked joint on the floor near the gas peddle

what we got here then ? he said ,bending down picking up the joint of ashes

you two get out of the vehicles now,he said to ching and foxie

the other officer started to walk around to the left side of curtis,s car towards the left back door and passenger side watching ching and foxie climb out while the other officer pulled himself back out of the car turning his attention to curtis

you have got some explaining to do,he said,placing handcuffs on curtis then asked him for his driving licence

it's in my glove compartment curtis instantly told him

while the other officer told ching and foxie to stand next to each other on the safe side of the dual carriageway while cars constantly drove passed curtis and the blue flashing light police car in the early afternoon of that day,the officer started searching and patting down chings clothing

empty your pockets,he said to ching,as ching listened to his instructions starting to take out whatever he had in his trousers and jacket pockets while foxie did the same putting whatever they had on the floor beside him while the other officer walked curtis over to ching and foxcie so the other officer could search all three of them while he went into curtis,s car through the passenger side door opening the glove compartment taking out a driving licence,he then went back to curtis asking him his name and address and D.O.B while curtis stood there next to his friends,curtis he realised he had a small plastic button bag in the back of his trousers pocket he was trying his best now to avoid the police from searching for he knew he had some cocaine inside of it but he couldn't do anything in trying to get it out from his pocket for his both hands were handcuff he stood there next to ching filled with worries answering the questions the police asked him giving his name address with D.O.B the police who asked him questions started started speaking into his small radio attached to his uniform near his chest asking for a radio check on curtis name to see if he was wanted by the police for anything as the other police officer was satisfied after completing the search on ching and foxie finding nothing illegal on them then started to pat down searching curtis.

have you got anything sharp in your pockets,he asked curtis

no officer was curtis reply as the officer stuck is hand slowly and carefully into curtis both front trouser pockets

they were empty

turn around he then said to him so he could search his trousers back pockets putting his hand into one of his back pockets pulling out the small plastic button bag

oh what have we got here then he said looking at what he now had in his hand

what's this he said again?,looking at curtis who stood there saying nothing just holding his head down looking angrily at the ground before him

it looks like class A drugs he said lifting the small back up in front of the other officers office

the officer who was waiting for a feedback from his radio

checked then started reading curtis his rights

you have the right to remain silent he said then continued on speaking until he finished the right speech then grabbed hold of curtis hands walking him to the petrol car shoving him in the back of the police car as the feedback for his radio check came through saying curtis was not wanted but was on bail and due to appearing in court in a weeks' time

that's no problem the officer then spoke into the radio we have just arrested him for possession of drugs we are going to be bringing him into the station right now over and out,he said looking at curtis,then slammed shut the police car door walking over to the other police officer who stood there waiting while watching

ching and foxie picking up their possessions they had taken out from their pockets from the floor

the officer came over spoke a few words to the other officer

then told ching and foxie whatever they had inside of curtis,s car they had best collect now because the car was going to be impounded they both had nothing inside the vehicle

well you guys will have to find your way home or to wherever you are going the officer said before he started locking up curtis,s car then the both police officer walked back to their police car got in shutting their doors

once again the officer used his radio calling for someone to come and pick up Curtis,s car while they both watched ching and foxie slowly walking away into the distance.

It was not long before curtis found himself locked up in a police cell spending the night then finding himself standing in front of the magistrates court judge the next day getting remanded into prison for 6 days before he had to attend a court hearing for speeding with possession of class A drugs and breaking is bail conditions everything happened so fast,one moment he was out having a laugh with his friends enjoying his freedom, the next thing he knew he was handcuffed standing there in front of the judge of the day who was giving him a 2 year prison sentence.

CHAPTER 20
ABERAVON BEACH

It was still Saturday the 20th of october in the evening hours bulla was sitting in the passenger seat of the dreads car, he had not long got back into the car after quickly climbing out to go back into his car parked right next to the dreads car to get the plastic bag filled with class A drugs from his glove compartment, he got back out his car closing the passenger door then jumped back into the dreads car holding the bag in his hand, where they were parked was in a nice secluded area no other vehicles was parked next to them on the beach road, it was on one of the few layby's that were to be found along the beach front where people would usually park their cars if they wanted a nice relaxing rest and a nice view of the sandy beach with the sea moving and waves with tides which would be easily noticed in the day times.

Right now it was too dark to see the beach with the sea from where they both sat, the both of them had only been parked up about 10 minutes in that time only a few stranger had walked on by pass them about 20 feet away on the promenade taking their slow paced promenade evening stroll, you could see them walking but you wouldn't be able to recognise their faces from where ryan and bulla was parked a little distance away because of the darkness of the early evening, the air was smelling fresh from the breeze which was blowing in on them from the sea front the dread had his driver side window halfway down allowing his nostril's to freely take in some of the fresh sea breeze, the window was also half down on bulla's side while they both sat there with no music on in the car.

The dread looked towards bulla then said,curtis said he would be about 15 minutes so he shouldn't be much longer now

So you say you got three ounces of the cocaine there ?

yeah dread,bulla said sitting there waiting for curtis who didn't live too far away from where they had parked he also knew exactly where they were parked having met the both of them at the same spot for the first time nearly ne month ago buying 1oz of cocaine from them so he could trade it on to his customers in and around Port Talbot

bulla had only met curtis once this was the last time he had bought the substance from them at the spot where they were now waiting.

you know what ?the dread said looking at bulla through his thick black framed glasses I'm going to need another ounce of that stuff for my mate colin in bridgend can you sort it man

yeah that shouldn't be a problem dread all I have to do is give my man up there in london a phone call and make the order

okay when can you do this ? the dread asked as his right hand picked up one single long thin black dreadlock out of the many which were laying there falling and flowing down from his head onto his lap starting to feel it gently with his fingers while he held his mobile phone in his left hand

you know what call him now he said,taking his mobile phone then started to press on a few digits

a few seconds later the phone connected then you could hear him saying

alright luis how are you brother

i'm cool bruv what's up everything good

yeah man all is good man bulla answered with a smile showing on his face then said you know we are linking up next saturday down my ends in cardiff with 3 more ounces but can you make that 4 instead

yeah that won't be a problem I will put the order through for you you know how much this will cost you don't you

yes man I know the money will be here waiting for you when you bring it down ok

yeah that's what I want to hear bruv luis said down the phone

okay luis next week then okay he said again before he disconnected his phone put it back into his jacket pocket then looked at the dread who was still caressing his locks

saying well that's sorted dread

nice one the dread said sitting there relaxed as they could now hear the loud roaring engine of a motorbike coming from a little distance away getting louder and louder until the motorbike came right up next to where they were parked pulling up right beside the dread's car on bulla's side they both looked while watching the rider dressed in all black leather biker's wear with a black motor helmet on his head with a black rucksack fastened tightly on his back turned off his bike's engine then looked towards bulla before taking his helmet off

alright boys curtis said with a big wide smile on his chubby face as he started loosening the rucksack taking it from off his back

what's happening he said as he climbed off his motor bike

jump in the dread said looking pass Bulla through the cars window at curtis

who walked a few steps then opened the back door on bulla side of the car with his rucksack now in his hand then jumped into the door.

Nathaniel.s. Bird

◆ ◆ ◆

CHAPTER 21
STAPLETON ROAD

Around the same time that evening in the Easton area side of bristol city alex was walking up stapleton road with a plastic carrier bag filled up with groceries inside he had just bought some caribbean food from some of the local shops,some salt fish fresh leafed spinach fresh callallo sweet potatoes yams green bananas butter beans with some fresh goat meat a bit of beef with some herbs and spices as he strolled on forward up stapleton road,he hailed saying hi to a few familiar local faces of people he knew he few black and white faces a few dreads with rasta's a few of the local working residents of the area with a few local down and outs who daily hanged around the long stretching road of stapleton road passing the few pubs on each side of the road where you would always see a few people standing outside talking with each other while drinking their alcoholic drinks while you passed some of the pubs you could hear reggae music playing in the pubs backgrounds which would be turned up much louder into the dark late hours on the weekends there was always an entertainment place to go in the easton area with other neighbouring area right next to it known as St Paul's they both had their fair share of black pubs where all races were welcomed to enter inside to listen to some sweet sounds of reggae music with R and B music and soul music with a little Bashment music playing in these both area's these where the black areas of bristol where you would come across a lot of jamaicans black british with east africans with somalin's every summer bristol would hold its carnival which would bring great numbers of people from all over england and wales to its bristolian street into the Saint Paul's area where it was held.

Alright alex a voice called out from across the other side of stapleton road where he was walking on the way back to his flat,he looked spotting the face of errol his older neighbour who lived in the flat upstairs above him,errol was just coming out from a off-licence store with a packet of cigarettes in his hand he had just bought,errol was born in jamaica he had been living in london for a few long years before he came to bristol.

Alex crossed the busy road when he found a space in the traffic over to errol then the both of them walked on up stapleton road walking towards the apartment of flats where they both lived,alex had been living there 9 years while errol had been there 8 years they both walked in through the big wide white doors of the apartment building both walking through the ground floor then unlocking the first set of security doors which took you to the first floor after punching in secret digits with letter's as alex got to the 2nd floor it was there he left errol to go to his flat while errol continued on up the stairs to the next floor to his flat,alex held onto his bag of groceries while he unlocked his door with his key picked up his groceries then walked into flat closing his door behind him walk on through his small hallway into his living room where his younger brother mark was sitting.

oh alright carl,he said,when he saw carl a white lad from port talbot sitting there on one of the three settees in the room

when did you come down then? surprise surprise he then said,standing there on his lime coloured carpeted living room with the bag still in his hand

I got here about 20 minutes ago on the train carl said,in a strong welsh port talbot accent nice to see you alex,he continued to say,then said,

do you want a spliff alex ?because mark just bought some weed with money I just gave to him.

yes let me just put these groceries away then I will join the both of you alex said,looking at carl and his brother mark who was sitting there on his big sofa rolling up a spliff in his black t-shirt with black shorts on wearing black sock with no shoes on with his mohican style hair head shaved on each side

yeah cool bruv,he said to alex ,

alex started to walk into the opened kitchen right next to the living room then started unpacking the bag putting the groceries away in the kitchen cupboards,while doing so he could hear a mobile phone ringing in the living room but continue putting away the groceries.

yeah alright I'm cool he could hear mark say

 after answering his mobile phone,I'm just chilling out up here in bristol

what you saying luis

I'm looking to be travelling out of london next weekend on the saturday I'm just wondering if you are going to be about

yes Mark answered,I will be here in bristol at my brother's place

okay mark I'm going to be passing around with my mate carlos okay.

As luis was speaking mark got up walked a few steps then handed the spliff of weed he was smoking over to carl then took his seat back again

nice one carl said as alex walked out of the kitchen

where's that spliff you promised me,he said walking over towards carl here make yourself one alex,he said,

putting his hand into his tracksuit bottoms pocket taking out a small plastic button bag which had a small amount of weed inside he then put it on the small pine wooden coffee table next to the chair he sat on which already had a packet of large size tobacco rolling paper on it with the ashtray with his mobile phone

no problem,alex said,standing by the coffee table picking up the rolling paper while mark continued speaking on his phone to luis.

Mark had known luis several years now at least 7 years,he first met Luis in his brother stephen's studio flat in edmonton angel back in the year 2012 then had not seen him again until surprisingly bumping into him in prison in the year 2014 when luis was serving a small prison term which was his first ever prison sentence for drugs selling and the time was not good on Luis behalf because he was under complete and total stress being recently transferred to this new prison from Pentonville prison in north london,he had only been in this prison a few days and was being bullied and targeted by a group of trouble makers who intended to make his prison life hard,luis knew at the time he had nowhere to hide,he could see no escape being a new inmate on the prison wing full of strangers he knew no one,he also knew trouble was brewing trouble which he just couldn't avoid not knowing what the out coming was going to be but also knowing by the looks of the situation he was now found in that it wasn't going to be a pleasant neither nice outcome,it was only just a matter of time he knew by the vibes he was feeling he was going to get his face smashed in by these few troublemakers on his wing,

He sat there in his cell on his iron bed alone worried thinking he may have to speak to the prison officers on his wing telling them he feared for his life was in danger wondering if he could be taken off the wing being be placed on another wing,when association time came around his cell door was unlocked,he didn't really feel up to going out onto the landing to join up with all the other inmates down the iron staircase on the ground floor he just sat there on his bed looking around his cell thinking while he sat there for a few moments listening to cell doors on his landing unlocking as the feet's with voices of inmates could now be loudly heard all making their way down the stairs his eyes looked at his big plastic mug,he then decided he would leave his cell and get some hot water from the big stainless steel urn on the ground floor regardless of those few strangers who had bad intentions for him for he needed a hot cup of tea,he was already sorted out with a lot of goodies in his cell,tobacco coffee powdered milk with a few packets of biscuits,he thought to himself, he stood up picking up his plastic mug from his small wooden three draw cabinet that he would get some boiling hot water then go straight back to his cell and slam his cell door shut spending the rest of the evening alone in his cell until another new morning started while he considered also reconsidered if he should speak with one of the prison officers on the wing about what was troubling his mind,he walked out of his cell closing his cell door a little not allowing it to close for it would instantly lock then could not be opened up again by him neither any other inmate only by anothe prison officer-,then walked slowly down his landing while having a look over it at the same time he was walking to see who was on the landing below him also on the ground floor, when he had walked passed a lot of inmates on his way to the hot water stainless steel urn standing in the queue waiting for his turn to use the urn after he poured hot water into his mug then turned around realising stephen's younger brother mark bird was standing a few inmates away behind him in the queue, he was surprised shocked stunned he felt an instant feeling of relief it was like he had just seen the light the dark strong thunderous cloud which had been lingering over his head for days had just vanished disappeared instantly dissolved just by seeing mark's face feeling his presence Luis felt empowered,Mark looked at luis then said, Luis what are you doing in here ?

Luis then explaining to him how he ended up in the prison system after mark had gotten his hot water from the urn,they walked through the wing taking a seat by the pool table,mark then telling him he had been transferred from a prison in wales today to finish the rest of his sentence in this prison, as they were talking another one of mark cousin who had been in this prison for quit sometime was walking through the ground floor of the wing recognised a big built muscle guy sitting near the pool table he instantly recognizing it was his cuz mark then quickly walked up to him

hay cuz how are you man ?

Mark looked up seeing leroy douglas his 2nd cousin from cardiff city standing there right beside him,no one attempted to bother neither trouble leroy in this prison he was to be feared he had a reputation in this prison with all the other prison's too in the 9 years he had been stuck in the prison system without being released he was on IPP and at this moment in time he was still stuck in the prison system not knowing as yet his E.D.R. date of release,the demon characters who were on luis back feared leroy they knew he wasn't a person to be messed with on the wing and he wasn't a small person standing at 6ft 2 inches tall 16 stones

When mark's eyes looked seeing his cousin standing right there infront of him you could see a big happy smile appear on mark's face thinking now to himself how fortunate he was to be sitting here with his cousin leroy and a good friend of his brother's luis because at the time he was happy in the prison he had served his sentence in down in wales where he was sharing a cell with bulla having strong support in that prison with his other cousin duke there also ryan the dread ,all of them together in that prison was a force certainly not to mess with it was when he was told only days ago he was getting a transfer to a prison all the way up in london his heart dropped he wasn't pleased with the news now knowing his prison visits would be ruined because now his visitors would have to travel to far to see him from port talbot and bristol secondly he would be leaving all his prison friends and his cousin becoming a total stranger once again in a foreign jail, so to be sitting here right now having his cousin standing right infront of him with luis beside him he couldn't believe his luck but more fortunate than him was luis and luis knew he was now more empowered also strengthened when mark's cousin leroy appeared on the scene,knowing now he had strong solid defence on his side.

As luis sat there he spotted francis with his two mate's walking towards him on the ground floor,when he saw luis sitting there next to mark and leroy standing right near,francis with his mates looked stunned shocked very surprised as he quickly walked pass not saying a single word.

It was only a week later mark moved from his cell moving into luis's cell with him'luis then telling him about the stressful days he had been going through with francis and his mates before mark had arrived to this prison,mark then telling luis not to worry we will find a way to smash those guys before I leave this prison putting them under some pressure just like they had you under pressure,that very same evening when their cell door was unlocked for the evening's association mark and luis went down onto the ground floor to the tv room taking their seats in the back row,a short time later leroy joined them,mark then told leroy what pressure luis had been under before he had arrived at the prison,leroy then telling luis that evening in the tv room when francis had thrown something at the back of luis's head he had watched it all happening for he was sitting just behind francis and his mates right at the back row,he told luis he also knew he was a new fresh face inmate to the prison wing and that he rated luis for being brave that evening by throwing the same item back at francis and his mates.

Yes leroy stated while looking at luis as he sat there next to him in the back row of the tv room that evening while mark listening on you were brave leroy told him then laughed,well what do you reckonedmmmark ?

he said,in a low tone of voice to leroy are you up for a little bit of fun as leroy looked on at him then said you know me I get bored easily so I'm up for any kind of entertainment cuz

okay then mark said as luis listened on that evening as mark and leroy sat there in the tv room talking quietly while laughing at times together as they both thought up ways were they could hurt francis and his friends.

Back at Alex's home in bristol mark had just finished talking on the phone to luis now sitting there comfortably on the sofas with alex and carl also in the living room.

CHAPTER 22
DRIVING ON

Around about the same time in the South of Wales ryan the dread was speeding along up the A48 motorway his foot was stuck hard down on the gas pedal speeding along in the fast lane being chased by his friend bulla who was right being him nearly bumper to bumper the dreads eyes quickly looked at his speedometer 113 mph it was showing as the rev dile was in the red zone moving further and further deeper into the red,the dread focused on what was now infront of him while quickly looking into the cars indoor front mirror seeing Bulla's car keeping right up with him,his car lights nice and bright in the dark evening g night cat's eyes glowed all along the carriageway filled with dazzling colours of white orange and red as they both drove towards bridgend town which was now only another 4 miles away.

After already covering 8 miles from port talbot where they had with 3 ounces of cocaine which he had put into his black rucksack while speaking to the dread for a few minutes in the back of the dreads car before climbing out going back onto his motorbike,Bulla and the dread watched him start his bike up then noisily rode away from aberavon beach out of their sight into the distance,now the both of them were speeding swiftly up there dual carriageway to bridgend,bulla was going to spend a little time with the dread there.

The dread started flashing his fog lights on and off as he quickly closed in on a car infront of him signalling warning he wanted and needed to pass it very soon,the car infront then quickly moving over into the middle lane,ryan kept his foot down hard on the gas pedal taking a quick look at the speed dile which was now moving up pass 120 mph then started flashing his fog lights again warning another car infront of him he needed to move pass looking again in his rear view mirror still seeing bulla right behind him not being able to as yet leave him trailing behind while his CD system was blarring out the musical tunes of *Frankie Paul* which filled his car the car in front ignored the flashing car lights of the dread causing the dread to slightly start lifting his foot up from the gas pedal the speed dile started dropping as the dread covered his brake pedal with his left foot gently tapping down on it.

Bulla seeing the dread's brake lights going on and off a few times instead of putting his foot down on his brake pedal,he smiled turning his indicator left light on then swerved his car at speed into the middle lane already knowing the lane he was in,there were no cars near behind him because of the speed he had been driving at trying to keep up with the dread also already seeing beforehand the middle lane he had just drove into was clear apart from the few cars in that same lane about 75 yards up ahead from him were he could see their back red lights,he pressed his foot down hard on his gas pedal then pressed his car horn hard as he sped pass the dread who was in the fast lane,taking a quick glimpse through his driver side window noticing the dread looking towards his left at him as he passed,bulla laughed to himself instantly driving passed the dread he drove into the slow lane which had no vehicles in for up to 250 yards avoiding having to slow down for these few cars already in this lane further up infront also avoiding the in-evitable of the car which was infront of the dread slowing the dread down avoiding that it may soon turn into the middle lane blocking his way putting him at high risk of a terrible accident,bulla drove on at high speed for a few seconds illegally passing the cars now in the middle lane before flicking his indicator back to right so he didn't have to slow down for the cars infront of him in the slow lane,speeding on back into the middle lane having already passed the car in the fast lane which has been slowing down the Dread slipping back into the fast lane from the middle lane ahead of the dread now pushing his foot down on the gas pedal even more seeing that the lane ahead of him was clear while watching his speedometer rise higher and higher leaving ryan the dread now trailing behind trying to catch up with him.

It was only a few moments before he came to the sign showing bridgend town was the next turning off the dual carriageway on the left,bulla took the turning then followed the signed route into bridgend town centre followed just a little behind by the dread they both were heading for the pub in the town called the Trump where bulla drove to pulling up parking his car in the pub car park the dread was soon to follow in parking his car next to bulla's car.

CHAPTER 23
ON THE MOVE

The musical sounds of *Mary J Blige* song, *you remind me* was playing through the USB stick connected to the music system in the car as it drove on through along with the moving traffic on the south circular heading towards the north side of london this early afternoon the clock on the dashboard was showing the driver the time was now 12.23 the south circular was very busy the lanes were packed with traffic everyone today like every other day seem to be having somewhere to go this afternoon even though the weather was looking miserable the sun had not come out this morning there seem to be no guarantee that it would be showing it's warm friendly face this afternoon the rains had not long ago stop falling leaving it's wet evidence all over the concrete roads with streets of london city.

The autumn clothing was now swiftly becoming a thing of the past days,you could now see the public people no more wearing tracksuit tops sweat shirts with light weight jumpers it was slowly approaching the seasonal time for thicker warm heavy jackets for the rains were now falling more regular while the climate was now on the decline the umbrellas of all different colours were now a must carry along item.

The driver could see out of his passenger side window as he stopped behinds several cars ahead of him who were waiting for the traffic lights to change to green a few people walking along on the pavement on his left wearing their rain-coats with winter jackets some wearing scarfs around their necks it won't be long before winter was here his thoughts told him as he could see the traffic light starting to change, within moments he was rolling through the traffic once again picking up speed rolling with the traffic flow now on the north circular the car he was driving was a new model ford focus,he had only just got on finance from a car company paying a small deposit then monthly payments for the next five years his old car he had traded it for scrap because of the problems it had been giving him constantly the last passing year he loved his old car but it was costing him unnecessary money so it had to go but this brand-new car he had been now driving only these last 2 months he loved it even more than his old car to be honest all the years he had been driving nearly 20 years now driving many cars this was the first ever brand-new car he had actually owned well once he had completely finished paying off all the payments that was but still for now he called it his own personal car which was now playing for him some nice music the music of the artist called *Dennis Brown's* song *If I had the world.*

He looked back at his dashboard while he drove on 12.47 the time showed i'll be on time,well it won't be late atleast,he thought leaning over to the left of his car,the traffic started slowing itself down again,the cars infront stopped for yet another set of traffic lights,his car came to a stand still,he quickly picked up a packet of cigarettes he had on his passenger seat right next to his cigarette lighter next to his mobile phone he slipped a fag out from the 20 packet dropping the box back on the seat slipping the cigarette into his mouth,his left hand reached for the lighter to put light to his cigarette placing the lighter back on the seat,he focused his eyes on the traffic infront which was just starting to move forwards once again for the light were back on green,taking a strong deep pull of his cigarette inhaling the smoke driving along slowly with the moving traffic,his ears took in the sounds of the music playing all around in in his new car,within minutes he found himself at a stand-still the traffic had stopped moving he looked ahead of him through his windscreen trying to see trying to figure out what the problem was because usually at this point on the north circular the traffic was usually flowing,all he could now see was a long row of cars with other vehicles lorries with vans all stationary all at a stand still.

bloody traffic jam,he found himself uttering,his left hand move towards the volume dile of the music turning it lowering the volume of the music just a little bit allowing himself to focus and think better, little by little every minute he found himself moving a little more forward in the traffic still wondering to why the traffic had suddenly gotten so congested,he looked at the time on his dashboard 12.57 it looks like I'm going to be late his thoughts told him now seeing himself sitting there in the traffic standing still looking down at his passenger seat at his mobile phone,he picked it up pressed a few digits then waited for the person on the other end to answered while he slowly edged himself forward in the heavy slow moving traffic,he could now see blue flashing lights of several sirens not sure whether they belonged to police ambulance or the fire brigade,it must be an accident he told himself,his car slowly moved forward holding his mobile in his hand switched onto loud speaker listening to it ringing away

hay mate i'm on my way,he said,as soon as his phone connected to the other side,

I'm just 5 minutes away but I'm stuck in heavy traffic

I think there's an accident that has happened out here on the north circular he stated as he spoke into his mobile phone

I maybe be a little late but I will phone you as soon as i 'm outside your place,okay,he said,before he disconnected the call,placed the mobile back on his passenger seat next to his lighter and packet of cigarettes, he continued to move slowly along with the traffic towards the blue flashing lights of the sirens approaching closer and closer until he could see a police motorbike with a police officer standing right next to it while it's lights flashed ,the bike was parked up in the right hand lane the police was directing traffic off that lane directing them into one single left lane as he drove forward into the left lane passing the police who was directing the traffic who stood to his right side,he could see a few more police cars with blue siren lights flashing and a ambulance with its back door opened the right lane was closed from there onward, he then noticed a white sheet covering the whole body of a person from head to feet so that no one could see the person not knowing whether they were male or female, a motorbike laid in the right lane all smashed up not to far from the dead person there was also a car next to the damaged motor bike which had it's back end damaged he noticed as he drove on slowly pass also noticing there were a few people standing near the damaged car and motorbike with the police officers,before he knew it his car was once again picking up speed moving swiftly once again in the traffic he was soon turning off the north circular driving down a few local streets heading into the Palmers Green area then driving through a few more streets until he arrived at his attended location parked his car then picked up his mobile phone pressed a few digits waited for the connection then said

hay luis i'm outside your place now

ok carlos the voice of luis said down the phone.

CHAPTER 24
AT HOME

Back in Edmonton Green just a few miles away from Palmer Green stephen had not long come in after picking up a few groceries from the edmonton green shopping centre,was now home alone in his living from tapping away on his keyboard working on his novel

book 3,Birdy the black guy from Port Talbot,South Wales,

he wasn't picking up his son Jaydon from his grandma's today which he usually did weekly or sometimes fortnightly it all depended on how he felt,he had already arranged he would be picking up his son tomorrow morning so he could spend a few hours with his dad.

As stephen sat there writing away his fingers tapping away selecting words forming words creating more written lines turning them into sentences while forming more chapters to this new book slowly watching it developed his mind was actively seeking out while searching and exploring more bright ideas with interesting thoughts,he constantly tapped away caught up now in his own private world of thinking thoughts,he had only started writing this new novel at the start of october 2019 on the 11th of october.

Writing seem to be his hobby it was always something he found himself doing when he had nothing important to do to pass away any empty time it was a time filler for him,he was only on chapter 24 but was satisfied on where he had already reach and how much he had already written since the 11th of october because inbetween the passing days with weeks of this months he had been out working for the security company as a steward of a few weekly days with one or two weekend working shifts at the wembley stadium where there was a big event for the NFL american football event the stadium was filled with over 60,000 people attending he also worked the shifts in an area called leyton once again at the tennis and Hockey Stadium as a steward one weekend of that month,jaycee also worked with him at this event.

That day he bumped into him in the event not seeing jaycee in person about 6 weeks,they both worked at a different event together a charity cycle ride event, where jaycee had picked stephen up that morning in his car driving him to the event which was a bit of a distance away although they had spoken many times with each other over their mobile phones, Jaycee had told him he would be working at the Tennis and hockey stadium at the end of october stephen telling him he would be working there also, but they had not arranged between each other how they were getting there, Stephen had taken the overground train from his area then caught a bus from hackney central to leyton to the event,thinking it a little strange how jaycee hadn't this time offered him a lift the days running up to the event neither did he ask stephen how he was getting there,stephen though thought to himself on the day travelling to the event that atleast he will get a lift back home if jaycee ids at the e vent,

yes he was working there from 11am to 7am at the event alongside stephen today but unfortunately stephen didn't get a lift back with jaycee for jaycee told him he had taken the public transport in to work today because his car had some battery problems he had to leave it at home,after their shift finished they both left the venue taking a bus back to hackney on the way Jaycee asked stephen if he had seen junior lately for he hadn't.stephen told him he had been around juniors home a few times this month speaking with junior about art exhibitions dates,junior had a art exhibitions just a few weeks ago in the beginning of october in hackney but stephen didn't go to the event but told junior that he will in time attend one of the other oncoming event and also introduce some of his own personal artwork there in time.

Stephen sat there that saturday afternoon in his living room all on his own tapping away on his keyboard watching letter after letter form into words then sentences then into chapters filled with eager anticipations and inspirations creating his adventure novel.

CHAPTER 25
REMINISCING

Luis was in his kitchen making a hot cup of tea when his mobile phone in his living room on the coffee table started ringing,he left his cup on the kitchen table quickly walked into his living room picking his phone up he was expecting a call from carlos so he thought it's probably carlos ringing,he was right seeing carlos name appear on the mobile answer screen,he stood by his coffee table listening to carlos saying to him he was only 5 minutes away but held up in heavy traffic believing there must be some sort of accident just up ahead of him but he was on his way before the phone went silent,he put his mobile phone back on the coffee table then went back into his kitchen to finish making his tea then came back into the living room taking his seat in his chair with his hot cup of tea in his hand by the side of his sofa there was a green rucksack where he had put a change of clothing with some toiletries with a towel inside,he was fully dressed in his jeans jumper with the sports trainers on his feet his eyes looked towards his tv which was switched onto the music channel the artist *Chris Brown* was being shown singing one of his well known songs *Loyal* while he danced around luis sat there drinking his tea while he watched the tv until he finished drinking the last drop of his tea from his cup got up walked back into the kitchen which wasn't very big in it's size leaned over his kitchen sink washed his cup clean then turned off the hot water tap placing the cup onto a plastic kitchen rack among a few other washed plates with glasses then walked back into his living room to the coffee table picked up his mobile phone then sat back down on his sofa again,his eyes looked across from him at the wall clock the time was just passed 1.15pm then his eyes moved towards the tv as he waited onto his mobile phone waiting for carlos to ring him,*Rhianna* was singing *Rude boy* he liked the music channel he would always find himself watching this channel when he was on his own if he wasn't watching it he would be listening to it from his kitchen or from his bedroom turning the volume up a bit higher so he could hear the music playing if he weren't chilling in his living room.

Luis was still single while living on his own which he didn't mind for now but hopefully not forever,he hadn't been in a long term relationship for years,just a few short term ones since leaving prison,he sat there waiting on carlos while his minds thoughts went back to his prison sentence term when his days were save by mark and leroy from the trouble-makers who were after his blood like thirsty mosquitos in a hot dry land hungry for fresh blood,francis knew the game had changed so quick without any warnings thinking while be-lieving he with his mates were at a great advantage.

That evening when the prison officers unlocked all the cell on the landing for association time francis walked out of his cell with his big blue plastic mug in his hand with his cell mate the both of them beaming filled with confidence springs underneath their feet's as they walked along looking for their other mate who was in a different cell on the same land-ing below luis when they both spotted their mate the three of them banded together walking down the iron stairs to the ground floor with a big grin on all of their faces laughing and joking with each other about how they were going to target luis while patiently terrorising him for their kicks as they walked to the steel hot water urn pouring hot water into their cups which already had tea bags sugar and powdered milk in them before they disappeared into the large tv room to chill for a little while before they would be getting up insearch for luis to start their intimidation games while sitting himself down with his two mates,he realised he had left his tobacco pouch in his cell telling his mates he would be back in a moment leaving the tv room walking on through the ground floor landing towards the Iron stairs pass the pool table on the wing.

As he was doing so passing a lot of inmates in their blue prison t-shirts while some had on their prison blue and white striped shirts his eyes spotted luis sitting down next to a black dude full of muscle a person he had never seen before in the prison who's this guy he thought as he walked closer knowing this black inmate was definitely a new comer and looked very intimidating like someone no one in their right mind would mess with he also noticed the black bad boy of the wing he knew as leroy but never ever spoke a word to him was also sitting there with luis as he walked pass them luis caught his eye he quickly looked away cowardly toward the direction of the iron stairs quickly walking up them to his landing on the 1st floor to collect his tobacco while now thinking to himself what the heck is going on who is this guy this new inmate luis was talking to while thinking it must be his new cell mate who just got into prison today it must be he thought oh well okay he thought pushing open his cell door which was already unlocked but closed in near to shut,we are going to have to lay low for a bit and see who this muscle black dude is maybe he might not even like his new cell mate no one has a choice who they are sharing a cell with when they first come in here he thought with a slight laughed pulling open one of the three draws of the small wooden chest of draws taking his pouch out from it,his thoughts then went to leroy but why is he there sitting with them he thought his mind starting to work on overtime trying to find some form of understandable answers to this new situation he had now stumbled upon,he slammed shut the draw feeling a little furious avery angry with the thoughts because he just didn't know neither did he understand what he had just seen,he slowly walked towards his cell door filled with thoughts and doubts feeling now a little confused also frustrated stepping out of his cell door onto the landing hearing the voices of inmates down below him on the ground floor playing on the pool table and playing the wooden table top football game with other inmates hanging around down there talking to one another he couldn't believe how the situation had changed just like that it was like he had nearly caught the rare precious bird but somehow it escaped flying away from the readily made set trap there waiting to snare it,how can this be he thought as he walked on down the iron stairs to the ground floor intending now to avoid walking close pass Luis this time but walking first to the right far wall of the wing where there were a few prison cell doors of inmates all unlocked a few inmates were still in their unlocked cells chatting with other inmates who had gone in to see them while there were a few loitering around idly on the ground floo, he walked pass,Luis Mark and Leroy were on the left to him when he had passed them earlier going to his cell now as he approached near to the pool table on the far right of the wings wall he looked towards the left to see what Luis was doing but couldn't see him realising he had disappeared he was no longer sitting there with the two black dudes,he continued walking on then walked into the big tv room filled with one hundred chairs ten chairs to each of its ten rows as he walked in his eyes looked towards his left at the back row

oh there he is Francis said to himself,spotting Luis sitting there in the back row talking with the two black inmates Luis looked towards Frances seeing him sheepishly walk onwards into the tv towards the front row to join his mates,Francis could hear the three of them laughing among each other in the back row taking his front row seat.

It was just a few more minutes before Luis phone rang, Carlos was calling him telling him he was parked up outside waiting for him,he left his chair walked over to his tv set turned it off then switched of the plug switch on the wall, then walked back to his sofa picking up his green rucksack from the side of it carried it in one of his hand has he left his living room going into his hallway taking one of the few jackets and coats he had hanging up there on wall hooks with him towards his front door he then quickly put his rucksack down putting on his waist length thick brown padded winter jacket on then picked up his rucksack opened his front door walked out shutting his door behind him right at the end of his front gate only a few steps away beyond the short size iron gate Carlos was parked looking at him from his driver seat.

CHAPTER 26   AT HOME

Stephen still sat there fully activated in his mind tapping away on his keyboard that early Saturday afternoon at home in his living room where he sat comfortably relaxed in his black Adidas tracksuit bottoms white t-shirt with his black sports trainers on his living room was nice and warm the only thing which could be heard was his fingers hitting down on the keyboard letters with the noise of the electric blow heater's noise buzzing away blowing out warm heat his tv was on with the volume pressed onto mute right infront of him was a large wide room window covered with a white netted curtain blue thick curtains on each side of the curtain rungs which were draw open the rain had started falling again this afternoon the weather was far from pleasant which was to be expected in this time of the yeah, he wasn't even aware of the weather conditions outside he wasn't planning, to go out anywhere until later this evening he would be, making his way by public transport to his partner Sarina's home until then he was caught up in the world of words selecting picking choosing developing creating while forming this new this new book now infront of his eyes using up the moving passing moments of the day as positively as he could by not wasting his time of day away he believed that all what he was doing right now every time he sat down infront of his computer in his living room or at Sarina's home and started typing he believed he was just patiently investing into his future plans every word he tapped into his novel was always one word away from the end of the book even though he knew he had a long way yet to go before it's ending also knowing in himself the book with all the other books with art drawings he had created would not be possible if he didn't use up the opportunity of any of his free time and if he didn't create free time for himself alone,he hoped though that one day in the future all what he was doing all what he was creating he may somehow make some money from it although writing was his hobby it was also something he intended in making money from it especially if you have already written over 47 small self-help books of knowledge including two novels this book he was now working on would be his third novel part 3 of Birdy the black gut from Port Talbot,so he just kept on tapping away on a personal mission on his agenda always finding time to walk on his project fixing up the little loose ends here and there tightening up the last few screws into his money making machine hoping that when it was the time to introduce his created inventions to the whole wide world it would be positively effective operating the way he hoped it would in slowly patiently bringing in the sterling's pounds dollars the GBP great British pounds so he could start climbing one step at a time up the fantastic splendid money ladder leaving those ruined empty desolate dark days of small change with a lot of empty pocket days right behind him.

All the things he was doing in the pass days weeks months years with decades was all a preparation for the moving in towards yes future days 2020 was just around the corner before you knew it Christmas day will be knocking on your door also New Year's Eve then it's the year 2020 the time clock was ticking it wasn't slowing down time was certainly moving on the battle for cash was raging there were many a casual of its roaring raging storms now to be seen as 2019 steadily moved those of the working class people were struggling even the benefit system was now being changed from jobseekers allowance to universal credit a new system now set in place for those or very low wages also for those who were unemployed a hard system it seem for all those who were used to the JSA system where you received a little benefit money once a fortnight, now the universal credit was paid into the banks of those who were on it once a month,if you were out of work running short of cash all the crisis loans which use to be available on jsa system in the earlier years which people were entitled to the maximum of 3 crisis loans within a year this had now been completely removed from the JSA system just before the uc had been introduced then activated, people only now being able to receive only one small loan in each calendar year, so now if you found yourself in crisis where you had no food no money. Well then there was nothing the benefit system could do for you and back you up only food vouchers for the food voucher store outlets now these were the days with times were you could not just allow yourself to lose focus.

Don't lose focus,should now be ringing alarm bells in your mind, it was now you had to know the way the better way or find a way a way to come off universal credit system, Stephen always believed nothing was impossible,you can get there if you try,he always told himself knowing, those who are determined will succeed,in the human challengers games of life ,which to him was not ,just a dream,not just a silly little game which you did not take seriously,he took it serious even though this was just, another day ,in the days of my life, I'm am going to ,stay focused ,he said to himself knowing he was on a ,treasure hunt ,while moving through ,this mysterious time ,experiencing ,troubles on every bend and corners,he sat there on his own constantly tapping away on his keyboard creating more new pages to his new novel as the afternoon time ticked on by,until his mobile phone rang,he picked it up answered the call saying hi Ashley my son how are you ,staying there sitting on his chair talking to his oldest son for a little while.

❖ ❖ ❖

0.27   ON A MISSSION

n Just over 70 miles away on the M4 motorway Carlos had just taken the turning off the motorway driving towards one of the many service stations you would find on its journey's route his petrol gauge was far from empty it's dile was just touching below the half-filled tank measure he was just feeling a little peckish a little hungry in need of a few snacks to munch on along the journey he with Luis was on their way to Cardiff the driving distance was just over 150 miles about a near 3 hours' drive from London

I may as well fill him up,he said,driving towards the service station

yes Luis said putting his hand into his jeans pocket pulling out his wallet while Carlos drove on towards the filling station parking up beside one of the many petrol and diesel fuel pumps then turned off his ignition undid his seat belt held onto his car keys

Here take this Luis said handing a £20 note to Carlos

no I'm cool you hold on to it he said,then climbed out into the wet rainy weather then opened the back door of his car grabbing hold of his long length light weight grey raincoat from off the back seat where Luis's green rucksack was with his brown jacket he had taken off along the journey putting it at the back by his rucksack Carlos started filling his tank while he watched Luis open the driver side door climbing out

i'm going to get me some munchies he shouted then quickly got his jacket from the back of the car shutting back the cars back door hurrying along in the rain while putting his jacket on going to the service station shop to get some drink crisps and chocolate with a sandwich in moments they were back on the motorway driving at high speed in the pouring down rain windscreen wipers flapping back and fro with the usb stick in the cars system playing *Fabolous* hit song *Into you* while filling their mouths with different flavoured sandwiches washing it down with fizzy drinks and juices before before moving onto their chocolate snacks while chatting away to each other.

Luis and Carlos had known each for a good few years now both were of Portuguese descendants both coming to London in their junior years their parents leaving their home-land of Portugal Luis's mother coming to London with him and his older brother and sister in the year 1989 after devor-icing their dad while Carols parents came over in 1990 they both came from different parts of portugal Luiss his parents came from Lisbon,Carlos his parents came from Setubal his parents still lived together in the South part of London in a area called New Cross.

When Luis was sent to prison in 2014 for his first ever prison sentence Carlos was always there for his sup-port attending the court with him hoping he wasn't going to prison,he was there,when the verdict was giving received a phone call from Luis asking him to break into his flat recover-ing drugs hidden in his wardrobe in his bedroom for him and if he could look after it,after Carlos had done what he was asked he kept sending Luis money into prison which was put into his private cash account which he could use in the prison on canteen days which came around once a week were he could buy himself all the prison comforts he needed Luis's cell was like a candy shop he was never short of anything never in need always being generous to his prison friends Mark and Leroy, Mark had no worries because he was Luis cell mate after being in prison only a 1 week Mark was already independent his private cash was already healthy from all the hustling he was doing in the Park prison in Wales where he had been transferred from this prison Leroy never even needed to ask for anything if he ran short of any items because he was always being offered things constantly from his cousin Mark and his prison friend even though he was making plenty of money undercover in the prison system.

Yes Carlos showed his loyalty all through Luis prison sentence even meeting him outside the prison gate on his day of release picking him up in his old blue honda civic car driving Luis to his home,there Luis phoned his mother telling her he was out of prison and with Carlos and he would come to see her later,they both chilled at Luis having a drink smoking zoots while catching up on lost time with his good mate.

Inside of the boot of Carlos car was a black and white sports bag which had 4 ounces of cocaine all in separate 1 ounce packets the bag was hidden underneath a load of Carlos clean clothes with other items there was also a black plastic electronic weighing scales in the bag he had told Luis the stuff was inside the boot under his garments Luis,had made a phone call not so long ago when they had started the journey out of London telling Bulla he was just leaving London with his friend and he would call him when he was not too far away from Cardiff it had taken them just over an hour to travel out of London onto the M4 motorway due to so much heavy traffic on the A4 route out of the city the time on Carlos car's dashboard was showing 15.50pm as the car passed a sign telling them they were now 20 miles away from Bristol and 65 miles from Cardiff to go Luis said looking at Carlos who was smoking on a zoot of the skunk weed which Luis had made 10 minutes ago smoking the first half then passing it over to his driver.

yeah we should get to Cardiff within the next hour maximum bruv,he said driving on at a sensible speed not breaking the

70 miles speed limit slowing right down from his high speed manoeuvre's reminding himself he had to be sensible and very careful knowing he's carrying a boot full of drug with him today to deliver to a customer he had only met once which was around a month ago he knew he was taking a risk travelling with that amount of drug also knowing if he got caught with it then it's straight through those tall high wooden prison gates it's there he would be going,he also knew at times in life you have to weigh up the risk taking a chance if you feel the odds didn't look to bad,at first when Luis had told him could he give him a lift to Wales to drop off the stuff he said no asking why don't the person come up to London and collect the stuff if he really wanted it, the person could even take a public coach up here and get the drugs he explained to Luis

no Luis had told Carlos,I've already told him exactly what your telling me but the person seem really paranoid Luis said at the time with a laughter

Paranoid of what Carlos questioned

he thinks if he travels all the way up here to buy the stuff from me he's going to get robbed,Luis laughed again then said like I'm going to rob him,no chance man that's not my style he continued to say

at that time on the phone at his flat while talking with Carlos,

he then explained to Carlos,he had never met the person called Bulla but was introduced to him by his old cell mate Mark,

Bulla was Marks old cellmate in the Park Prison in Wales in 2014,

Mark had phoned Luis asking him if he could do him a favour by getting a quantity of cocaine for a friend of his in Wales

that's no problem he told Mark

But there's one problem Mark then told him,that person

wanted the stuff but wasn't willing to travel to collect it and he would have to do the travelling

Luis at that time told Mark he would have a think about it and get back to him very soon,he did the next day in the evening he phoned Mark after talking with Carlos on the phone Carlos eventually agreeing to do the journey to Cardiff after weighting up all the benefits think well we can make some easy money Luis was going to give Carlos a good amount of money for driving him up there and back home,they had already done one trip all things went smoothly with no problems no troubles no worries Bulla got what he wanted he was happy with it and they got the cash the drive back to London was even better as Carlos pressed his foot down hard on the gas pedal travelling at high speed in the darkness of the night knowing now his car boot was clean free from the class A drugs easy earned money,he thought,speeding back feeling happy so Carlos was willing to travel again to complete mission number 2 and now they both were just less than an hour away from meeting up with Bulla for the second time as the car casually cruised along on the M4 motorway heading towards the big huge long seven bridge which separated England from Wales having the english channel flowing below it's tonnes of solid steel.

CHAPTER 28
THE WAITING GAME

Back in South Wales in Port Talbot town Curtis that early afternoon was on his mobile phone talking with Ryan the Dread while he sat on his toilet seat with his toilet paper roll in one hand the phone was on the toilet floor on loud speaker

yeah Dread I'm really running down on low I only got a few wraps of cocaine left just a couple of grammes is your friend coming today I hope so I got a lot of people relying on me in m y town

I spoke to Bulla yesterday,

he said he's going to be coming sometime today, right now I am waiting on his call to confirm everything when he calls me I will get back to you right away

so just chill out until you hear from me !

okay Curtis said before his mobile on the floor went silent

The dread who was 12 miles away in Bridgend town

he had called Bulla's mobile yesterday morning asking about if his delivery he was expecting tomorrow was still coming, he got a positive feedback hearing Bulla's voice saying the running was still on he will be getting his delivery tomorrow I will call you as soon as I am sorted was the last words he spoke to Ryan the Dread so all through today the Dread kept his phone close to him waiting on Bulla's phone call while he chilled out at his home with his partner, this little running was just a finger in one small pie for him he would make a quick earner from Curtis for setting up the deal for him,he made sure Curtis didn't have Bulla's contact number so every time he set up the meetings he would receive a big drink for it having already told Bulla never to give his contact number to Curtis before they both knocked fist together with a big smile on their faces even though Curtis was getting good quality co-caine weighted right to the fair balance Curtis was also happy with what he was getting knowing he was getting a good deal even making good profit from selling all his deals.

Everyone was on a winner no one losing out,he was also waiting on 1 ounce of cocaine to be delivered to him from Bulla this evening which he was going to hand straight to a mate of his,so there was a finger in each pie quick money he thought to himself playing the middle man making the con-tacts without even having to hold onto any drugs or be around the drugs for to long,it was just that one phone call he was waiting for all morning and now it was nearing the evening hours the afternoon was fading away fast while he sat there on his sofa in his living room with his woman beside him watch-ing with their little child, the tv she wasn't aware of what her partner was up to he never involved her neither did he let her have any idea in how he made his money he just told her not to worry i'm not robbing anyone and bringing any trouble to our home i'm just hustling I know people who are very usefull were the only words he would tell her,since he had been out of prison a few years now not a single police officer had come to thier home her trust in him had strengthened as the ticking of time had move along it's passageway, she had been with Ryan many years now meeting him one night in the days gone by in a nightclub in her home town bridgend were she was born and grown up

It was the usual saturday night she was out on the town to letting her ,long brown hair down feeling free with all her girlfriends she was out having fun dancing the night away in a nightclub called The Benz it was very busy filled out packed with clubbers she had arrived there just after 11.30pm with her friends after drinking a load of cocktail with shots of spirits in the other pubs in the town while enjoying the evening passing along,when she got to Benz with her friends she went to the bar to get herself a drink finding herself standing next to a tall dark stranger with long dreadlock,he was there pondering and waiting for his drink,he looked at her then smiled,she smiled back while thinking it was nice to see a black person in her town for 99.9% of the town was filled with white people there were only two black families that she knew in the town when this tall black stranger turned to her then smiled he then said to,her whatever you are buying I am paying for it in a London accent it made her even more interested in this black stranger finding herself feeling very curious of who this person was and where he was coming from,he paid for the drink then told her to come and sit beside him

i'm with my friends she said

well bring them along with you he told her as he stood there beside the bar

okay she told him

the next moment she was walking over to where the Dread was sitting with his friend Birdy in the far dark corner of the club where he told her he would be ,this was in the year 1995 way back in time, the Dread had been loyal to her staying with her through-out the years it was over 20years they had been together now and she knew him well even though in every relationship you always get ups and downs they had their problems but they both had ridden through the turbulences with storms together getting through their troubles, even in his prison time in 2014 she had stuck tight and very close to him writing him love letters every week also sending him money whenever she could and whenever he asked her if she had it,the dread had served his prison sentence for a GBH charge since he had been out of prison he had been moving much more carefully because he now knew also realised he had responsibilities his woman and child the dread sat there beside his woman on the sofa watching the tv waiting for a phone call from Bulla the time was moving slowly passed the afternoon hours to early evening he didn't really want to call Bulla again the dread just sat there with his mind filled with thoughts.

Curtis had finished his toilet duties he was now flushing the toilet pulling up his pants then he picked up his mobile from the toilet floor turned around looked in the toilet bowl making sure it was clean then left the toilet walking through his upstairs landing then down his red carpeted staircase to the downstairs department of his three bedroom council house

I just come off the phone to the Dread he said to Reeko as soon as he walked into the small back room of his home who was standing by the back room's window sill breaking up the fag he had in his hand then placing the tobacco parts into the rolling paper,he had been at curtis home since early this morning hoping sometime today his friend will be getting a fresh delivery,he was hoping it was today for he already had his own plans set for later in the day later tonight infact where he would be trading some of the stuff he would be buying from curtis in one or two of the nightclubs in the town tonight it was where he made his quick sales quick money,the last amount of cocaine curtis had gotten from the dread ,reeko had bought a quarter of it from curtis and had gotten rid of all his stuff in a space of 3 days Friday, Saturday and Sunday over one weekend then came back buying another quarter of the stuff trading this to his friends in the town throughout the week days with the last bits he had left on him the following Friday in the clubs it was all finished and his wallet was fat,he was hoping curtis got his delivery sometime today because he was ready to go again.

So what did he say reeko asked ?

standing there by the window while he picked up his cigarette lighter from off the window sill then the small block of ash which weight about 2 grams putting the lighter flame to it heating upon the ashes which he was now holding between his two fingers looking,while standing now in the centre of the room then moved his eyes back to the ashes turning off the lighter flame walked back putting it on the window sill then pressed the ashes with his finger crushing it in then breaking off small pieces crumbling it as it fell apart in-between his fingers into the rolling paper filled with tobacco making sure the ashes lined up dropping neatly into the paper from one end to the other

oh the dread's going to call me back as soon as his mate calls him,he's waiting on his call he said,taking his seat in the small back room picking up his own packet of long silver rolling paper

chuck us a bit of that ashes then reeko,so I can make myself a spliff,he said watching his long-time friend rolling a joint of ashes infront of his view.

CHAPTER 29
ON THE MOVE

Carlos had driven pass the toll bridge on the seven bridge now driving pass the sign which said in a Welsh spelling welcome to Wales,he pressed his foot down a bit more harder on the gas pedal speeding on forward picking up speed watching the speed dile rise back up to 40 mph 43 mph then further after moving slowly behind a load of cars with lorries on the toll bridge point keeping in the slow lane while watching the speed dile quickly rise up to 70 mph keeping now cruising in the slow lane at this speed towards Cardiff city,Luis had taken his mobile off his lap while Carlos drove on then pressed a few button waited for an answer his eyes looked at the cars dashboard clock time 16.21 it was showing

hi you good Bulla,he said

hearing bulla's voice saying,how are you Luis,

yeah i'm not to far away from you now,we have just passed over the Seven Bridge and now entering Wales so I will be in Cardiff in about 40 minutes,I will meet you outside that pub in the docks again okay

alright I will be waiting outside in my car see you then okay he said,then dis-connected,

luis put his phone back on his lap then looked out the cars windscreen pass the windscreen washer which were moving

back and fro rapidly keeping Carlos vision clear seeing all
what was happening infront also ahead of him,the rains were
still falling the roads were soaked with rain water every time
Carlos found himself driving behind a large vehicle a lorry or
a coach he would speed up driving into the faster lane overtaking then moved back into the slow lane again because of
the sprays of rain water splashing all over his windscreen from
the vehicles his car front lights were switched on because the
light of day had now turned fairly dark even though it was
barely early evening.

Only forwards was his destination to Cardiff city so he
could make for himself with his friend some easy cash the
battle for cash was always against him but he knew he was a
real challenger in the warfare which was do or die the cow-
ards always died for they never ever take chances,it was about
chances you win or lose with the chances you take it's all just
a chance but you had to be wise enough knowing when to
take your chance he wasn't driving all the way down to Cardiff from London on a joy trip oh no this was certainly not the
case, he needed money he wanted to see gain if there was no
profit in what he was doing then he would not be interested in
even attempting in giving it a try for to Carlos it was all about
achieving or forgetting and leaving searching for better ways
to line his pockets his foot was firm on the gas pedal keeping
it on the 70 mph limit while his mind was on reaching his destination of buke town the docks area in Cardiff city.

CHAPTER 30
WONDERING

Ryan the dread sat there on the sofa beside his woman and his child his eyes were fixed on the tv but his mind was very far away from what the tv had to offer after he had looked at his wristwatch seeing the time was 4.45pm he started feeling a bit annoyed his own mind had been telling himself to phone bulla for the last hour and fifteen minutes but he found himself silently battling with his ownself in telling him not to make any calls to him but have a little patience and if Curtis called him to just let it ring out and don't answer any of his calls until he had heard from Bulla first.

Ryan didn't like delays although he already knew it was a thing always to be expected,it was nice when things ran smoothly and people were on time punctuality reliability where there was no stress even if there was a delay then please give us a ring mate and let me know what's going on,commonsense he would always think for it's exactly what he would be doing if he was on a running's with someone if something got in his way to hold him back delaying things he would be straight on the blower to the person he was doing business with letting them know what was happening but right now bulla had him in suspense he had the Dread waiting don't keep me hanging Bulla,were the thoughts circulating the dreads mind,while he sat there with his woman and child he couldn't help keep looking at his wristwatch every 5 minutes after the time had passed 3.30pm until his woman said to him, what's up why are you keep on checking the time looking at him through his framed glasses trying to look into his eyes,

he shrugged her off a few times then he got up from the sofa going upstairs into the bedroom shutting the door behind him laying down on his bed not being able to help looking again at his wrist watch the time had just gone 4.20pm his one hand started feeling some of his long dreadlocks which flowed pass the side of his face down pass his shoulder's down to his chest to his waist as the thoughts of his mind was stuck on Bulla thinking of what he was up to and where he was holding his mobile phone in his other hand,it started to ring Ryan pulled his hand up to his face looked at his phone to see who was calling him about time he told himself when he saw the name flashing,

hay what's up he said as soon as he answered

yeah dread things are going to be running a little late but everything's cool let your people know you will have the goods about 7pm I will be by your home around 6pm okay

okay that's good news the dread said I will be waiting for you Bulla okay

no problem Dread Bulla said before he cut himself off from the phone.

CHAPTER
31   AT HOME

Stephen had been in all day still tapping away on his keyboard having no intentions of allowing anything to get in the way of his spare time he had little intervals where he would get up go in his kitchen making a quick sandwich with a cold drink then it would be straight back to typing,it's not every day he had plenty of free time to catch up getting on top of any of his personal projects but whenever he found the time he would fully take advantage of it even doing overtime on it,for he knew it was personal investments in his own personal time which was very precious to him.

He did receive a call on his mobile mid-afternoon not long after talking with his son Ashley around 2.45pm from Jaycee asking him if he was interested coming with him to Bristol city this evening he was going to drive there in his car because he had now fixed the battery problem buying a new battery,Jaycee had a woman down there he would go visiting every other week who he had met in the Bristol carnival this year when he went there with Birdy Eden junior she was a 28 year old black british woman who originally came from Hackney east London but moved to Bristol a decade ago.

Jaycee was a little older than her and a little younger than birdy when he asked birdy if he was interested in coming for a ride to Bristol this evening and stay there until Sunday evening birdy turned the offer down telling Jaycee he was busy working on his project and maybe next time, he then went straight back to his typing away keeping his fingers on his both hands actively tapping away allowing the words to flow add up multiply creating more and more chapters to his new novel knowing time was of the essence and waited on no one being fully aware this year was slowly moving on coming to it's end 2020 was on the horizon.

CHAPTER 32
THE INFORMATION

After receiving the news from Bulla the dreads felt good glad to of gotten the news he had been waiting on all afternoon he sat up on his bed after the call then called curtis to give him the news that he will be in Port Talbot by about 7pm this evening he then left his bedroom going back downstairs taking his seat back on the sofa with his girlfriend and child knowing bulla will not be at his home until another hour and a half.

CHAPTER 33
THE SWOOP

The dash-boards time showed 16.57 when it arrived outside the Baltimore pub in buke town Cardiff docks area Carlos pulled the handbrake up turned off the ignition while Luis held his mobile phone to his ear after calling bulla's phone number

we are hear Bulla he said, as Bulla answered

okay I'm on my way I'm only 2 minutes away he told him before disconnecting there were a few male figures standing by the entrance of the pub talking to each other in the dark evening the rain had stopped falling but the roads were wet the streets were empty around buke town the weather must of chased the people from off the streets music could be heard coming from the pub they were parked outside off reggae music you could hear the heavy bass beating vibrations the rhythms giving little life to the evening hours around here.

carlos eyes looked into his rear view mirror noticing the front lights of a car approaching

I think that's him coming behind us he said to luis

as luis looked around behind him

yeah that's him luis answered

is he with anyone, carlos asked

after having a good look watching bulla pull up behind carlos car luis could only see bulla alone in the car he's on his own he said turning around looking at carlos wait there luis said having his seatbelt already undone as soon as carlos had parked the car the music system was also turned off as soon as carlos switched his ignition off luis open the passenger door climbed out into the evenings cold air without his jacket on which he had long ago taken off after he had got back into the car after buying a load of snack with soft drinks at the service station earlier on their travels putting his jacket back in the back seat of the car next to his green rucksack so too did carlos,Luis walked to bulla's driver side part of the car bulla winded down his window staying there in his car

hay luis my bro,tell your driver to follow my lead,I'm going to driver to the entrance of the park it's just up the road which will be much safer to do the deal okay

alright luis said before he quickly walked back over jumping into carlos car,bulla started to slowly drive pass carlos follow him

he's just going around the corner to a safer place he told carlos

ok bruv carlos said,then started up his car moving on forwards following bulla through a few streets in Buke town until they arrived at the wide concrete entrance of a park which could not be easily notice as a park entrance in the darkness of the evening but the lights on bulla and carlos car showed the wide black iron gates to the park entrance which was still wide opened they drove through,bulla parked up just inside of the car park of the park,carlos pulled up beside him,the park seemed empty there was no one to be seen walking around which was a good thing bulla turned off his ignition climbed out of his car with his bag around his shoulder shutting his car door then walked over to carlos car as luis turned around in his seat watching bulla open up the back door of carlos car

just push my jacket with rucksack to one side,he said to bulla as the door opened bulla did so quickly picking them up putting them a bit further in the back seat of the car near to the door so he had room to sit down behind luis shutting the door behind him with his man bag around his shoulder

you got the cash ?luis asked,looking around at bulla from where he sat

yeah man it's all in here he said,holding his man bag up then letting it fall back down onto his lap

okay carlos said give me a minute the goods are in the boot,he then pulled a lever underneath his steering wheel to unlock the boot then unclipped his seatbelt opened his car door while his engine was still running with the car gear in the neutral gear handbrake safety on pulled up climbing out walked over to his boot opened it up then pulled his sports bag out from underneath a pile of clothes then closed the boot,his eyes swiftly scanned all around the darkness of the park with it's entrance to see if there was anyone watching him or coming his way there was no one he made his way back to his opened door jumped in closing it

hold this,he said to luis,placing the sports bag on luis's lap,luis's seatbelt was undone,for since following bulla through the few streets to the park he hadn't bother to put it back on when they started to follow bulla

carlos hand reached up turning the cars indoor light on just near the rear-view mirror so they had got light in the car,bulla opened is bag taking out a lot of paper notes from inside of it

there's 4 grand here,he said to luis and carlos,who's going to count it

luis will carlos said just give us a moment,he continued saying while he opened up the bag on luis's lap taking out the black electric weighting scales

hold this he said ,then turned his attention to bulla

pass the scales over to him

bulla quickly putting all the notes onto his lap noticing what carlos was about to do then took the scales from him putting it on his lap then picked up all the paper notes once again waiting to hand it to luis or carlos watching from where he sat at Carlos taking one block of cocaine out of the bag which was wrapped up in clingfilm

give me the money Luis said to bulla I will count it

here you are bulla answered passing all the notes in 4 separate bulks to luis as luis turned his body around in his seat with the sports bag still on his lap here's one carlos then said turning a little around in his seat handing bulla one packet to weight,

bulla turned on the electric scales placing the packet onto it weighting it

yeah that's bang on 1 ounce,he said,here's a next one carlos said,taking it out from the bag handing it over to bulla,his eyes looked out of the car all around him for a quick few seconds to see if anyone was out there watching,nothing out there things seem safe he thought to himself while luis sat there counting the cash keeping his two hands down as low as possible by the side of the sports bag on his lap,bulla weighted the 2nd 3rd and last one, they all weighted the accurate weights

alright the cash is all here bulla could hear luis say while he was putting all the cocaine away into his bag then zipping it up

i'm going to put the cash in here luis said quietly to carlos opening the sports bag on his lap putting all the cash inside of it

here are your scales bulla said holding it in his hand passing it over to carlos

thanks man carlos said taking the scales from him giving it to luis putting it into the bag zipping the bag on his lap

okay guys i'm off I will call you in a few weeks if I need more okay,he said as luis and carlos looked back at him sitting there at the back with his man bag strapped over his shoulder

yeah give me a call when your ready luis said then stretched his fist out knocking it against bullas now stretched out fist

bulla and carlos also knocked fists together in a form of re-spect before bulla left the car.

CHAPTER 34
ON THE MOVE

After bulla had driven out from the park entrance he turned on his music system feeling now in good spirit getting his delivery from luis then turned the volume up on high the artist known as Popcaan could be clearly heard by who over he drove pass in the now very quiet area of the streets of buke town out towards the city centre Popcaan was singing his song called,Dream, while bulla rocked his head up and down to the music enjoying now the passing moments of the evening,he then turned the music volume down on a low volume so he could make a call to the dread taking his mobile phone out from his dark blue sleeveless body warmer he wore a white tracksuit top underneath his body warmer with white tracksuit bottoms on with blue Nike sports trainers taking advantage of the red stop lights at the traffic lights he put his phone on loud speaker resting it on the passenger seat next to his man bag filled with drugs his eyes looked ahead of him at the few cars infront of him while he waited for the lights to change back to green his ears listening to the ringing tone,the city high streets were very busy even though the roads with street pavements all looked drenched soaking wet from all the earlier falling rains,crowds of people could be seen walking along this early evening busy popping into the many clothes shops gadget stores pubs,coffee shops with restuarants with many other shops to be noticed in the built up busy shopping area of the city centre,it was here the traffic slowed down a lot due to the traffic lights every couple hundreds of yards away until you started driving further away from the city centre

bulla's ears listen on until he heard the voice of the dread say yes bulla are you on your way yet?

bulla took his handbrake off pressed his gas peddle down allowing the clutch peddle to rise up under his foot when he saw the lights change to green

yes dread i'm just heading out of cardiff right now I should be in your street by 6pm okay he said as he followed on with the traffic flow passing the well known cardiff castle right there in the city centre looking spectaculer,magnificent okay the dread responded I will see you soon then,okay dread bulla said then disconnected the call as he drove onward and outward to the A48 motorway turning back up his music enjoying his ride to bridgend town.

CHAPTER 35

MEETING PLACE

While bulla drove onwartds to bridgend carlos was driving over the seven bridge aacross the english channel leaving the country of Wales behind them in and out of this country in such as shore space of time the car dashboard was showing the time of 17.53 it was only 5 minutes ago luis had come off the phone speaking to his old cell mate mark asking him where he was and that he was not to far away from bristol city

mark telling him he was in the city centre of bristol and Luis could meet him outside the MC Donalds store giving him the directions with street name to where it was, after going into the McDonald store while he spoke on to luis as he walked up to the counter buying himself a burger and also his friend carl from Port talbot who was still in bristol a burger with fries getting the receipt while he held luis on the phone then gave luis the post code to the MC Donald restuarant

okay I will be waiting outside Mc Donald's he told Luis he now stood outside with carl both about to eat what he had just bought telling carl after he had finished speaking with luis that luis was an old prison cell mate of his who lived in lon-don but was now coming to bristol from wales after visiting a

friend

he's going to be about 20-30 minutes he told carl while they both stood outside by the door of the Mc Donald's

carl look at his friend then said alright

luis memorized the post code then tapped it into his mobile phone map app,setting up his navigator system while carlos drove on across the bridge quickly closing in on bristol city which was only several miles away then started directing carl while he held his mobile phone in his hand all the way to the Mc Donald which took no more than 20 minutes to get there seeing Mark standing outside the talking with a white fella.

CHAPTER 36
CHANGE OF PLAN

At the same time back in edmonton green stephen was at home now sitting in his kitchen at his kitchen table eating some salt fish with fried dumplings and planting he had quickly rustled up together,he had been typing pratically all day non stop just trying to always get ahead of the game of his project investing in his own personal futuristic runnings so he hopefully would not be finding himself falling behind in time for no one know's what holdback can appear on the pathways of their lives to suddenly hold them back that they can't even find the time to do the things they want to do this was why stephen always tried staying ahead of his game always investing when he could make personal time it was something he never forgot.

while he sat there he thought you know what I might as well go with jaycee to bristol this evening give himself a little break from the typing because he had already put a few good hours work into his new novel he felt satisfied in what he had done he was now hoping jaycee had not yet left london for if so then he would of missed out on a oppurtunity,he left the kitchen going back into his living room picking his mobile phone up from the glass coffee table stood there,he called jaycee's phone number then waited for an answer

alright birdy,jaycee said

yeah cool jaycee have you hit the motorqway

no i'm still at home but will be leaving soon in the next 10

minutes infact he said

well I have change my mind come and pick me up,I will follow you to bristol jaycee if that,s still on

yeah birdy,no problem the time is now 18.10,I will be at your home by 7pm ok

nice one stephen said before he ended the call,he then started to change his clothing and putting his place in order before jaycee arrived.

CHAPTER 37
REMENISCING

When carlos parked up on the side of the busy high street main road outside the Mc Donald restuarant in bristol city centre luis opened the car door called out to mark beckoning him over to the car he turned himself around then quickly pulled his passenger seat forward knowing mark was a fairly big lump size kind of a guy then stepped back from the car,he could see mark with his friend walking towards his direction luis said jump in the back guys hold on a second though,he said as mark and carl were only just a few feet away,he walked to the back of the car opening the door pulling out his jacket and rucksack with carlos jacket,

okay you guys can get in now he said climbing out from the car

how are you mark bruv,he said,holding onto the stuff he took out as mark now stood right beside him

I'm cool luis things good man

okay i'm going to put these in the boot can you make your friend sit over the far end you sit behind me okay,he said before walking to the boot of the car which carlos had unlocked while sitting there parked up for those few moments luis put everything he had in his hand into the boot then shut the boot while mark and carl were now both sitting comnfortably in the back of the car with the back door closed carl jumped back into the car moving his two feet over the sports bag which had the scales with cash inside which was now down on the floor were he kept his feet,he shut the door then instantly picked up the sports bag putting it on his lap.

where we going then carlos asked luis seeing luis was now putting on his seatbelt,carlos had never met mark this was the first time he had ever set eyes mark and carl he had heard about mark knowing who he was through the many stories luis had spoken about mark he seemed like a good prison friend to luis from what luis had spoken about him,it was also the first time luis hads met mark in bristol since leaving the prison system even though they both had meet on a few other occassions since their release from prison meeting at Stephen's place when mark came up to london to visit his older brother,luis and carlos both didn't know carl he was a complete stranger to them they had never heard his name mentioned before.

Even carlos mind were filled with luis's prison memories of the time when luis told him the story about when mark and his cousin leroy activities defending him in the prison system the evening when francis walked back into the prison tv room noticing luis sitting in the back row with mark and leroy his blood went cold while walking to the front row to join his friends as mark leroy and luis watched him walking pass them,they all started laughing among each other while planning francis downfall,leroy was saying he wouldn't mind doing a few weeks down in the segragation block for that idiot i've got nothing to lose,he said looking at mark and luis,I don't even have an EDR date yet, i've been in this system many years without being released so it would be nice for me to release all my stored up anger on his face with my bare knuckles,he saids clenching his fists holding his both knuckles up infront of his face looking to his right at mark who sat next to him then at luis who sat at the end,leroy smiled at both of them keeping his fists up in a boxers fighting style then continued to say don't forget I may not even get caught and he will be way to scared to grass on me,also you cuz you can't afford to be losing any prison time standing infront of the prison governor you only got a short time left it's not worth your risk

I know what you are saying leroy you could hear mark say, while he sat there in the middle of them on his wooden chair

I would love to apply some pressure on his brain though just for some entertainment while passing this slow moving prison time they could hear mark saying as the three of them laughed again between themselves,so what's the plan then mark said being a bit more serious this time when he spoke looking to his left at his cousin leroy,

plan what plan leroy said sitting there with a curious smile showing on his black round face,plan he said again the second time I don't need no plan leroy said,when I see him out there on the wing later on or maybe tomorrow or any time,i'm going straight up to him and tell him I want a word with him in the toilets whether he likes it or not then he will know what time it is,it's that simple I don't beat around the bush,you know me cuz,prison might be wasting my time away but still when it comes to doing things I got no time to waste so let's continue allow the evening to happen we will see what developes leroy said then just layed back into his wooden chair looking towards the big tv screen.

as these memories also filled carlos mind of what luis had been telling him about mark and his cousin leroy,luis turned around to mark sitting behind him direct us to where you are staying at your brothers then mark

okay drive straight ahead he said to carlos directing him here and there while luis introduced mark to carlos

nice to meet you mark carlos said focusing on the road ahead of him then said with a little laugh inbetween his words i've heard a lot about you ,how is your cousin leroy ?

take the next left then drive straight ahead,oh my cousin he is still locked up in the prison system he said after hearing what carlos had asked him.

okay hope he's out soon man he's been in there a long time man

yeah mark replied I will be glad to see him touching back down on the roads you get me,he said,carlos drove on while carl sat there in the back seat silent but listening to all what was being said,mark introduced carl to luis and carlos as they drove along through the streets of bristol now entering the easton area where alex and mark lived.

CHAPTER 38
SPEEDING ON

Stephen was ready when jaycee parked up outside the front of his home then phoned him telling him he was outside

okay all good stephen told him,be with you in a minute walking to his main front door opening it walked out then closed it behind him,the only thing he had in his hand was his mobile phone no bag no change of clothing just his phone as he walked over to jaycee's car,jaycee sitting there watching him coming to the car,

get in rudeboy jaycee cheekily said with a loud voice then laughed,so it's bristol for the evening rudeboy,he said,watching birdy climb into the car shutting the front passenger door,

nice and clean in here birdy said,looking around making himself comfortable in the passenger seat,

one thing with jaycee he always keep his car immacculate and clean

what do you mean,jaycee said,have you ever seen my car filled with litter,not me he continued saying,pressing his foot on the accelarator peddle speeding off out of birdy's street doing a wheel spin

whats the rush birdy uttered,Bristol ain't going nowhere

jaycee just looked at him then smiled,knocking up the gears speeding on through the city roads brightened up by red yellow and green traffic lights here there and everywhere showing he had no time to waste always over taking any car which was in his way always trying to finds a way of getting ahead of the traffic on every given occassion while his left hand worked furiously through the gear stick changing them rapidly speeding onwards then suddenly slowing down before he came to speed light camera's with other secret hidden one's,he knew the roads of London well.

Birdy loved speed when driving but he realised jaycee was much more in love with speed ,now birdy didn't mind speed as long as it was his hand on the steering wheel and not another's,now he found himself in Jaycee's car driving through london city traffic rapidly on the way to the M4 motorway while they both listened to the musical sounds of *Mighty diamonds* singing the song w*hen the right time come* a short time later they were driving at high speed down the fast lane of the M4 like a bullet shot out from a gun,jaycee pushing his car as close as he coluld to it's limit.

CHAPTER
39 BULLA
AND THE DREAD

A little while earlier that same day Bulla was driving into the street where ryan the dread lived,he parked up as usual in the street keeping is headlight with ignition on he could see the dreads car parked outside his home he was parked just a few cars down,he phoned the dread telling him he was outside while he sat there with one of his hand feeling his blue cap covering his head

yeah i'm on my way to you the dread said,before bulla placed his mobile phone down into his lap,winding down the driver side window to halfway position,he had put his man bag filled with cocaine on the floor by the passenger seat which he was now leaning down towards picking it up by it's long strap pulling it up to him holding the bag in his hand he put the strap over his head passed his neck onto his shoulder,the dread opened up his home's front door stepped out closing it behind him dressed in a long black leather jacket which dropped down passed his knee wearing black jeans with thick black boots on his feet made of leather holding his mobile phone in his hand,he walked towards bulla's parked car his dread locks fully exposed dangling down long locks flowing while he walked with no hat on his head

you got everything he said as he walked right up to bulla car window looking in at him through his dark glassess at him sitting there

yeah it's all here bulla said,sitting there patting his man bag in his hand near his lap smiling at the dread

okay lets go and quickly drop 1 ounce off to my mate Ccolin then we will go and deliver curtis his lot

the dread then walked over to his car just ahead of him bulla watched him opening his car jumping in watching the dreads car lights turn on at the turn of the ignition key instantly the voice of Bob Marley could be loudly heard singing his song,Blackman redemtion,before it got lowered to a sensible volume,the dreads car started to move slowly out of the street bulla now following behind the dread,while the dreads fingers fumbled through the music list on his cars music system searching for a different tune to play,its time to play some Dennis Brown tunes which now could be heard playing inside his car the dread now stepping on his gas peddle speeding up the car travelling to his friends in chelsea avenue only a few minutes away.

CHAPTER 40
ON THE GO

The cars time was showing 21.15 when the car passed the sign saying 4 miles to the city centre speeding up even more knowing it was now closing in on it's destination instead of slowing down while the cars ahead quickly turned themselves over to the slower lane as they noticed the lights blinking and flashing rapidly tellling them this driver needed to move pass them

I will follow you to your brother's flat first you could hear jaycee's voice say

yeah okay birdy said,sitting there smoking a roll up of tobacco while listening to DMX singing one of his songs

yeah that's if anyones home birdy continued to say while watching the tobacco smoke as he blew it out from his mouth I just don't know why you don't just phone alex or mark so they know you are coming ,you crazy man jaycee said,speeding on down the dual carraigeway

not really birdy,said I just thought this time let me surprise them and catch them off guard

well I hope there are in for your sake birdy because your homes not just around the corner

birdy looked at jaycee then said

take the slip road on the left pointing his hand which had his roll up in it to the direction he was telling jaycee to drive towards,it will take you straight towards Easton,we aint going into the city right now he continued saying

ok jaycee answered flipping the left indicator lights on driving off the fast lane into the slower lane getting himself ready to take the left turn off the carraige way

anyhow if my brother's are not in i'm following you bro birdy said jokingly already knowing that if he couldn't get hold of his brothers jaycee wouldn't just let him be left stranded,he then said don't worry I will just buzz the older man errol upstairs and chill with him for a bit if they are out

jaycee kept quiet with a smile on his face as he turned left driving on towards easton before they knew it they were parked up outside the apartment building alex lived in

check and see if they are in I will wait here jaycee said leaving his keys hanging in the ignition as stephen opened the door smoking the last few pulls left in the small roll up between his fingers closing the door,the air that hit him felt cold due to him being sitting down in the warmth of the car for the last 2 hours and a bit jaycee didn't even stop off at any service station on the journey to put fuel in his car he drove straight to Bristol no stopping no messing about,stephen walked the few steps to the main entrance of the huge building apartment dropping the small finished roll up onto the cocncrete car park walking forward right up to the entrance walking near he could see someone sitting down on the small wall by the entrance,it was a resident who was known as black's he was one of the neighbours living on the same floor as his brother in the building

alright blacks,stephen said walking up right near to him

hi you alright your back down again from London

yeah man have you seen my brother about

yeah blacks said me did see them both earlier in the day but not since then they should be up there blacks then said cool black,stephen said before walking to the intercom a few more steps away pressing his brothers flat buzzer number into the system then listened to it ringing.

CHAPTER 41
A NEW MEETING
PLACE

The dread and bulla were both sitting on the sofa in the small backroom of curtis home they had got to port talbot on time meeting curtis at the same place on the aberavon beach front curtis turned up on his motor bike a few minutes after recieving the phone call from the dread telling him he's waiting at the beach front for him at the same spot,curtis turned up on his motorbike telling the dread to follow him to his house it would be okay for them to sort the business out at his place

okay the dread said then follwed curtis,bulla following behind them both,the time clock was ticking it was now 9.20pm they had been at curtis for over 2 hours everything was cool though curtis was happy with his 3 ounces of cocaine weighting each ounce on his own scales even though he was told by bulla they had already been weighted and was bang on point.

curtis still weighted them all just for the sake of it already knowing the last lot of stuff he had got from them were all on point and the stuff was of good quality no complaints from any of his customers only good positive feedbacks

it's why he thought to himself let me invite the dread and bulla in for a quick drink of some brandy and sort the business out here because they both seem cool to him.

the dread and bulla had never been to his house before the

only reason was not to do with trust but they had never ever even asked like the had no interest in knowing where curtis lived they just came down got their delivery done then disappeared out of town.

the dread had a couple shots of brandy mixed with coke,bulla had the same with a few spliffs,Ryan the dread sat there in the small back room feeling a little tipsy off the drink,his long leather jacket he had taken off hours ago was hanging on the corner of the rooms door,the door opened inwards,bullas sleeveless blue body warmer was on the arm of the sofa there they were the dread and bulla had all been talking the dread telling curtis that he was pretty good at trading the cocaine to his customers and whatever amount of the stuff he needed then it would be there for him in any amount if the cash was there for his mate bulla had great connections,

there's plenty of money to be made if you play your cards right

curtis listened on sitting on a small chair across from his visitors near the window in the room every time he looked at the dread and at bulla money making came into his mind,

just keep up the buying from us the dread told curtis it's only good quality class A we trade you know this for yourself plus your getting a fair price but if you can take more we will give you a good discount ok the dread said sitting there on the sofa

okay boyo,curtis said,sitting across from his dealers

well we are going to have to leave you know the dread said standing up feeling nice feeling merry from the brandy shots shaking his head to the left and right allowing his long locks to shake all around sliding one finger on his hand up towards the bridge of his nose pushing his black glasses closer up towards his eyes then looked at bulla sitting to his right who was now getting himself up while grabbing hold of his body warmer on the side of the sofa

yeah curtis we will see you again soon bulla said,

the dread took his jacket from off the corner of the rooms door before stepping out into the hallway,curtis was now on his feet following behind bulla who was now in the hallway walking near the dread the both of them putting their jackets on in the hallway as curtis passed them walking to his front door at the end of the hallway opening it for then then stood by his front door to see them off

alright curtis the dread said,walking up to Curtis then stuck his fist out towards him both knocked fists in a form of respect then the dread stepped outside waiting for bulla who did exactly the same as the dread before leaving curtis home.

curtis stood there at his front door watching the both of them walking down his front drive opening the little gate then closing it behind them both walking to their cars just parked right there outside

bulla then turned around saying,curtis you know what?

whats that he said in a loud voice

Ive left my man bag in your back room bro.

CHAPTER 42
EVERY ONE

No one wishes to be living with no money

everyone is out trying to earn achieve

some paper cash

the hustlers will be out there

constantly husling

for they wish to be living a life

which is fine fitting also fat

Some people take risky chances

because they wish to see their money grow

they wish to be seeing it grow very fast and swift

they dont want to be seeing it growing very slow.

Life for the working class is never easy

its far from neat looking sweet

when they are constantly working from 9 to 5

from 5 to 6 days of every moving week

The hustlers will still keep on hustling

while the workers go to work every working day

nothing though is guaranteed for all those hustlers

but guaranteed are all the workers pay day

Is it right what those hustlers are doing

is it injustice is it completely wrong

evereyone has to find a way to live

right below our daily rising sun.

The dread wants a big huge large fat bag of money

bulla wants big amounts in his man bag too

Curtis he is counting on relying on them

the trading of cocaine is bringing plenty of paper money into their view.

Will they keep on hustling the class A drugs

will they ever live and learn

if you keep playing with deadly dangerous fire

then i'm sorry to say one day

you will get caught out then be badly burned.

CHAPTER 43
WONDERING

Stephen stood outside the intercom listening to the number he had pressed into it ringing he waited until the ringing stopped then pressed it agaiin listening to it ring again until the buzzer stopped

they are out his thoughts told him,turning around in the cold air he could see blacks sitting on the wall with his thick warm winter jacket on looking comfortable in the cold evening air,

it looks like my brother's are out stephen said to blacks as he walked pass him

yeah man blacks said looking at stephen,blacks then nodded his head up and down

yeah laters,stephen said walking on quickly back to Jaycee's car,climbing back in,they are out he said,closing the door cutting off the cold air now sitting back in the warmth

so what are you going to do ?jaycee asked looking at him,

birdy then pulled his mobile phone out his front jeans pocket

i'm going to call alex and see where he's at

okay jaycee said,reaching his hand out to his keys in the ignition touching feeling then playing with them with his fingers like he was soon to be turning his ignition back on in a few moments while birdy called his brothers phone,waiting for it to answer

alex,stephen said

as soon as alex came on the phone,saying alright stephen

i'm outside your flat i'm in bristol where are you,I just been pressing on your buzzer

oh your in Bristol okay i've only just left my flat,your friends has come down from London we are with them now in the Three Black Birds pub

friends ? stephen asked curiously and a bit surprised

who,what friends are you talking about then,he instantly thought of eden,then said is it eden because 99% of the time Eden would come down to bristol from london.

no came alex's response it's luis,he's down here with us right now with a friend of is named carlos

oh luis and carlos thats a suprise,what brings them all the way here to bristol,he said to his brother

hold on stephen,luis is here he wants to speak to you

then luis voice came on the mobile phone while birdy sat there in the passenger seat of jaycee's car as jaycee looked down at his fingers fumbling with his ignition keys

birdy how are you bruv luis said excitedly,come now to where me and your brother's are

then birdy could hear luis's voice urging alex to tell him what the name of the place was they were all at.

CHAPTER 44
GETTING TOGETHER

Alex had only been in the Three Black Bird's 5 minutes when stephen called his mobile phone,he had just left the bar with a pint of guinness in his hand when his mobile in his jacket started to ring,he quickly walked pass a few strangers to the table in part of the place they were all sitting around,

Mark sat there with his alcohol drink carl sat next to him luis with carlos on the same table right across opposite to them alex took a seat next to his brother mark putting his pint on the table then took his mobile phone out his jacket looking at who was phoning him,

oh it's stephen,he said loud enough for everyone at the table to hear his voice through the reggae muisic playing at a high volume

stephen ,mark replied

yeah I wonder what he's up to alex said,taking a seat next to mark answering the call

alright stephen,he then explained that luis and carlos was with him,the next thing luis asked alex to pass the mobile to him as luis stretched is hand across the table taking the phone in his hand then started speaking to stephen

alex told luis the name of the pub they were in,stephen had no problem directing jaycee to the place knowing exactly where it was,having lived one whole year in bristol city in the year 1999 when he moved out with a friend from hackney east london named clarky,roger clarke

within 5 minutes jaycee was parking his car in the Pub's car park locking up his car as the both of them walked into the pub jaycee had sent a text message to the woman he had came to visit telling her he was in bristol with his friend birdy and he would update her on what time he would be coming to her home,he done this while stephen was outside alex's apartment building listening to the ringing buzzer,jaycee's lady texted him back straight away saying she was at home waiting for him to come around whenever he was ready for she would be home alone all night he didn't tell stephen anything about the text it was unneccassary

jaycee didn't know luis and carlos,he had never met them both neither had he heard birdy ever call or mentioned their names,so when he mentioned their names in his car while talking to his brother,Jaycee didn't know what was going on in the 5 minutes drive to the pub

stephen explained to him who luis was,how long he had known him and how he got to know Alex and Mark.

As they met everyone at the pub table stephen introduced jaycee to luis and carlos also to carl who was mark friend also a friend of the family,a part relative to roy bird the brothers older brother then they both took a seat on the table right next to the table the others were using,there they listened to music while talking and buying a few drinks,

jaycee had only bought one drink while he stayed there for around 1 hour carlos only drunk a little knowing he had responsibilities as a driver.

Jaycee left stephen there at the table,leaving to go and meet up with his lady telling stephen he would call him sometime tomorrow

A short time later they all decided to go to a carribean restaurant in the Saint Pauls area to all have a meal paid for by the expenses of luis and carlos,who stated they had earned some good money today but didn't tell any off them how they had earned it and the total amount of cash they were carrying with them they firstly made the decision carlos should park his car back at the car park at alex's apartment then they could all enjoy a good night out with plenty to eat and drink

okay I don't mind carlos said while he sat there at the table,

so alex went with carlos while the others waited in pub until they came back by foot only a 10 to 15 minutes walk back.

CHAPTER 45 BULLA AND THE DREAD

That same evening bulla went back and got his man bag from curtis back room of the house then he and the dread drove their cars out of curtis street then drove through port talbot town finding their way back onto the A48 the dread driving back to bridgend to his home carefully feeling rather tipsy of the alcoholic shorts with spliffs,bulla following him into his home where they went into the living room following him into his home where they went into the lving room his woman was upstairs in the bedroom while his young child was now in bed fast asleep

bulla had his man bag strapped over his shoulder the dread telling him to take a seat on one of the two armchairs while he took off his leather jacket walked out of his living room into the hallway putting his jacket on a tall plastic coat stand which had a few other coats and jackets on it belonging to his woman and child then wallked back into his living room,bulla was sitting down with his man bag on the floor by his feet,he was bending down over it taking out a load of paper cash putting it on the carpeted floor

the dread took a seat in the sofa just across from bulla looking through his black framed glassess at him taking out the cash then said

how muich you got for me this time?

a warm friendly happy smile could be spotted on his face as he started playing with the flow of dreadlocks dangfling down from his head passed his shoulders resting on his lap

bulla looked up quickly with a smile then looked back down at some of the notes he had just taken out from the bag leaving much more in the bag,then still bending down he started to count what was on the carpet

as the dread got up walked out the room into the hallway to the coat stand going into his black leather jacket,pulling his brown wallet out which was loaded with papernotes then went back into the living room putting his wallet on the coffee table infront of his sofa taking his seat once again the dread was given his portion of money from Colin earlier that evening for the 1 ounce of cocaine he delivered to him

well here's your share bulla said,standing up leaving his man bag by his seat on the floor with some paper notes on the carpet beside him.

here is your cash,he said putting the money on the table next to the dread's wallet

the same as last time bruv bulla said then turned back to his bag of money picking all the money up putting it in his bag zipping his bag up,turned around towards the dread who was now leaning out of his seat stretching over toward the money bulla put next to his wallet

bulla placed the strap of his bag over his shoulder

okay dread i'm heading home we will link up again soon

okay bulla the dread said leaning back into his chair with the wad of cash in his hand

you know they way out see you soon then he said as he started to count the money.

CHAPTER 46
OUT ON THE TOWN

The nights moon had finally completed it circuit now removing itself withdrawing its silver round face away from mankind,the late dark hours of the night was now being transformed from darkness to the early morning light the streets all around easton in bristol city looked desolated the streets were empty very quiet in most parts all the saturday night ravers having finished their saturday night drinking and dancing through the night hours were now wrapped up nicely in their beds catching upon the loss of sleep,if you were to see anyone out on the streets this time in the early morning lights would be more than likely female prostitutes young and old white and black hoping to get lucky getting atleast one more punter one more customer whether it was for a big or small job a sexual favour every single paper note to them added up most of them had cocaine and herion with crack habits you would mostly find them standing near or not to far away from the 24 hour off liscence shops there were more than a few who worked the streets in bristol traading their bodies for money.

little by little the morning drew on the daylights getting brighter the darkness disappeared a few cars drove through the easton area though sunday would be a quiet day all around bristol,mst high streets shops in the city centre would be closed the pubs in the easton area would still opening their front doors to all the public at 11am per usual.

At Alex flat he was fast asleep in his bedroom mark was in his room sleeping on his bed carl was on a blown up green air bed placed on the floor in Marks room near Marks bed ,carl was out for the count

in the front room stephen laid fast asleep stretched out on the living rooms sofa near to him on the floor there were another two air bed luis was sleeping on one of them carlos on the other on the carpeted floor there was a green rucksack next to luis opened up exposing clothes right next to the ruck sack laid luis his sports trainers was in the small red carpeted hallway which was surrounded by four white doors,the front door to the flat the bathroom door where the bathroom and toilet and washbasin were then alex bedroom door Marks bedroom door then the living room door the kitchen was only to be seen once you opened the living room door it was on the right to the room it didn't have a door it was a opened kitchen.

luis jacket and carlos jacket hanged up on the coat hooks which were in the small hallway were all the footwear and shoes with trainers were

carlos his bag with all his belonging were in the far corner of the living room where he was fast asleep on his air bed right next to him you could see the clothes he was wearing yesterday neatly folded up beside his sports bag

the flat was quiet the time was only 7.39 am in the morning they had all gotten back to the flat at 4.45AM,spending the night down in the city centre visiting a few wine bars then ending up in one of the big night clubs after filling their belies with some delicious carribean food,jerk chicken brown rice and peas with callallo and some salads in the caribean restuarant in St Paulls after spending a few hours in the city centre night club

they all strolled out the club around 1.45am walking into st pauls ghetto area checking out some of the black clubs listening to reggae music R and B also soul music while luis and carlos freely spent supplying everyone alcooal everyone had a good time until the last song was played inthe club then they all took the 25 to 30 minutes stroll back to alex flat now its there they were all now fast asleep as a new day was naturally on its way.

CHAPTER
47   JAY

Jaycee had been up wide awake and out of his girlfriends bed over 1 hour now,she had made him a lovely breakfast with a hot cup of coffee to wash it all down with,the time was just passed 10.30am sunday morning right now he was back upstairs in the bathroom after just finished using the toilet flushing the chain behind him,he stood there looking into the wide bathroom mirror at his arms chest and shoulders just quickly privately checking out his profile,he was pleased with what he saw standing there smiling at himself,his 17 inch bicepts broad shoulders with 50 inch chest made him look physically fit,he knew it and so to did his new partner as the thoughts came into his mind,he smiled at himself in the mirror again wearing his white vest before leaving the bathroom going back downstairs to join his woman who was sitting at the pine wooden six seated kitchen table drinking a glass of orange juice

do you want a glass babe ? she said,as soon as Jaycee entered the kitchen

yeah I would love some of that stuff,where's the clean glasses he said hearing what she juast asked him

you just sit down babes I will sort it,she said,putting her nearly finished glass of orange juice down on the table next to her finished empty plate of breakfast

jaycee's empty plate of breakfast was still on the table with his knife fork and coffee cup with small traces of coffee left inside of it

fiona walked over to the fridge,jaycee took back his chair at
the breakfast table she took out a large container of orange
juice placing it on the table infront of him then walked over to
a cupbboard right next to the fridge opening it up taking out
one of many glasses fronm the top shelf

jaycee looked on

so thats where all the glasses are hidden he jokingly said,sit-
ting there at the table with his black trousers on with his
white vest the kitchen temperature was warm due to the kit-
chens hot rings being on for the atleast 10 minutes while fiona
was frying up some breakfast

yes this is my glass cupborad she replied closing the cupboard
walking passed jaycee to the kitchen sink on the other side of
the table turning on the cold water tap giving the glass a quick
rinse turning off the tap then placing the clean fresh glass infront of him

there you are babes,fill your glass she said

while she took her seat back at the kitchen table across from
him watching him pouring the juice into the glass

so what time will you be picking your friend up from easton
she asked as he took one big gulp of his juice leaving the glass
now looking half emptied

I don't know yet i'm in no rush I will just chill with you my
little shortie until he calls my phone

fiona was only 5 foot 2 inches a little pocket rocket fascety
type of lady it was the reason jaycee loved calling her my little
shortie

well we might as well go back up then stairs so I can give those
muscles of your a little massaging she said looking across the
table at him now taking a sip of the juice this time from the
glass smiling at her.

Birdy the black guy from Port Talbot South Wales {book 2}

CHAPTER 48
THE MORNING AFTER

It was just before 11 am movements could now be heard in the bathroom at alex flat a bit of coughing here and there then a bit more coughing until the noise of vomit hitting the toilet water in the toilet bowl then a bit more loud vomiting could be heard again then a bit of moaning and groaning before the vomitting started again the commotion woke alex up from his sleep

the toilet wall was connected he shared the same wall with the toilet bathroom

mm,someones having a bad morning he said to himself,even though he weren't to sure if it was morning or early afternoon but he felt like he hadn't been asleep that long still feeling very tired,

he could still hear the noise of vomitting as he turned his head around on his pillow in the fairly dark bedroom of which the thick brown curtains were tightly closed,he pulled his quilt over his heads feeling comfortable and warm trying to enter back into the sweetness of the dream world once again.

.

Mark next door was also woken up by the loud vomiting noises coming to him which seem to be from the bathroomn slowly in as tired motion roled himself over looking down on the floor near to his bed seeing carl laying fast asleep with a some what slight smile on his face like he was being entertained by a lovely dream

well mark thought to himself,well it's not carl but I do wonder who it is thats vomitting away in the bathroom before rolling himself back over into the position he was already in before closing back his eyes drifting back off to sleep.

in the living room next to the kitchen at the far end of the living room near the window you could see the air bed which Carlos slept on,you couldn't see his face if you walked into the room only the back of his head as he laid there sleeping away in peace,there was only one person missing in the room,it wasn't stephen who was still stretched out on the sofa but his eyes with ears were both opened being woken by the noise of luis loud vomitting noises his airbed was laying there without him laying on it

      I hope he's alright stephen though after hearing luis vomiting on and off for about 5 minutes,he got up off the sofa opened the living rooms door walked to the bathroom's door stood in the small hallway by the closed bathroom door

hay luis he said knocking on the door hearing more vomitting noises coming from the bathroom

you okay in there

uuhhh I'm okay the voice of luis said I will be alright in a minute birdy he said as he was bending leaning over the toilet on his knees in his multi coloured boxer shorts in his socks and yellow t-shirt about to voimit again

alright i'm only checking on you,Stephen said

ok thanks birdy I will be out now he heard before walklng away from the bathroom door walking back into the living room laying back down on the sofa on top of the light sheet instead of covering it over him this time

alright birdy he heard carlos voice say,looking over from where he was towards carlos who's head was slightly lifted up from his pillow turned towards his direction

yeah carlos i'm cool,I just woke up birdy said as the both of them could now hear the sounds of loud vomitting

who is that vomitting carlos asked as he laid his head back down onto the pillow still feeling tired but relaxed his eyes looked towards the closed curtains which were drawn shut infront of him the back of his head now turned towards birdy

ho it's luis I just went to check on him in the bathroom,he's spewing his guts out man I think he must of drunk to much last night

oh is it carlos said laying there eyes still towards the curtains as a slight smile appeared on his face which started getting bigger and wider which Birdy couldn't see

the reason for carlos smile was because of the old memories that appeared in his mind of the last time he got totally smashed on alcoholic drinks waking up with a stinking ter-rible banging hangover which seemed to last forever this hap-pened quite some time ago several years ago infact he had gone out with luis selling a load of drugs,cocaine in the east london area while trading the drugs making themselves a load of money that night he was also drinking shots with other different strong drinks while going from winebar to wine bar trading the drugs he and luis made a lot of money that night he had a great night but the morning after he remembered and he will never ever forget taught him a lesson which was to never go over your own drinking limit also to be careful not to mix your drinks to much drinking anything and every thing for it will come back and bite you it will give you a nasty bite

that morning he realised he had bitten off way more than he could chew he had the biggest hangover of his life waking up that next morning in luis mums home were luis was living at the time waking up on the settee in luis room at the back of his mums home where luis had his own single bed in,it was back and fro to the toilet for him all morning accompanied by a terrible headache,he violently vomited out his guts in luis downstairs bathroom worse still luis mother was in the kitchen right next door who he couldn't avoid for you had to go into the kitchen from luis room to get to the downstairs toilet while he was vomitting he knew his friends mum could hear him he also knew she was probably laughing her head off at him loudly vomitting feeling as sick as a pig,feeling a little ashamed when he came out the toilet finding her standing there in the kitchen looking at him but she was understanding because she had a glass of water in her hand with a few pain killer tablets waiting to give to him without him having to say a word ,he took the glass of water with tablets then walked back into lui's room feeling sick closing the rooms door behind him looking at luis fast asleep in his bed looked snuggled up and cosy like he had not a single care in the world sleeping away like a little baby cuddled up nice in a warm cuddled cot

while he felt like he was locked up in extreme punishment in the chambers of horrid hell,he slumpped back into the soaf holding onto the glass of water with the two tablets already in his mouth washing them down with the water then dropped the glass onto the carpeted floor stranglely thinking to himself at that time while he struggled turning his head towards luis looking at him wondering to himself while hoping also believing that luis would more than likely be waking up feeling just like him or even worse for luis had drunk as much as him last night and even more also mixing his drinks,these thoughts some what made carlos feel a little better in himself for a few moments hoping somehow these thoughts would ring true for then he wouldn't be trapped in this hellish situation all on his own but may be able to share this punishment with luis,

moments later the feeling of wretched sickness with the feelings of vomitting took control of him once again causing him to quickly get up rushing out of the room through the kitchen,luis mum had gone from the kitchen he was glad not to see her there running back to the little toilet closing the door filling up the toilet bowl with vomit once again before sadly returning back to his resting place after flushing the toilet feeling weak and miserable while luis laid there on his bed in lovely comforts with the sweetness of peacefull sleep embracing him,

a little while later that morning luis started to stir in his sleep slowly waking up causing carlos to look over to see if he will be feeling totally ruined like himself the next thing he knew luis was quickly out of his bed rushing to the toilet without saying a single word to him

not even a good morning carlos,oh well carlos thought laying there on the sofa like a wounded victim of the passed weekend ,well atleast i'm not on my own now feeling like this join the club luis,he thought laying there barely able to move feeling totally destroyed for the last passing hour,it was less than a few minutes luis was walking back into the room closing the door

hay morning carlos you awake,standing by the sofa looking down at him

yeah bruv how you feeling luis,he asked as he laid there

i'm cool just woke up with a mouth filled with phlem bruv

had to spit it all out in the toilet bruv,luis said while carlos looked up at him looking fresh faced and happy

you look like the pits bruv,luis told him while he stood there looking down at him

yeah bruv,I feel like it to,I got a banging hangover bruv

luis offered his friend another glass of water with more headache tablets picking up the empty glass dfrom the carpet refilling it again giving it to carlos that morning with more tablets leaving him laying there waiting for recovery time to come appear and set in for him

carlos didn't get his wishes that morning hoping for luis to wake up feeling sick like him,in all the years they knew each other drinking together it was the first time luis had ever seen carlos in the state he was in this morning because of a drinking session the night before,while carlos had never seen luis in such a way,he had always thought since that morning a long time ago he wished the roles were reversed and it was luis being sick in the bathroom this morning and not him.

now this morning at luis friends brothers,alex flat,he laid there on the airbed just waking up from sleep hearing Birdy say to him luis was in the bathroom spilling out his guts being violently sick carlos couldn't help himself but to stare at the curtains infront of him with a now even larger smile on his face before concealing and hiding it turning himself around to his side then getting up sitting on the airbed looking across towards stephen laying on the sofa with his face towards carlos direction

how long has he been in there ? carlos asked now sitting there with his long hair lookiing a little tangled and messed up while dressed in his yellow vest his both legs out of the blanket wearing some long knee lenght yellow shorts

about 5 minutes I would say birdy answered laying there on the sofa in his black tracksuit bottoms and black t-shirt

oh he will be alright once he gets all that vomit out carlos said with a little giggle

you got any tablets there he then asked birdy,for I recxkon he's going to be needing a few with a glass of water

stephen got up saying he will as alex okay walking to the living room door disappearing out of carlos sight into the hallway he was back in less than a minute walking straight into the opened kitchen carlos looked on in the fairly dark living room that late morning back the thick coloured curtains were closed blocking out the daylights from entering in stephen shuffled through one of the kitchen draws then found a packet of Ibufen tablets filled a small glass with some water then went back into the living room placing the packet of tablets with the glass of water on the small coffe table to the left of the room near luis airbed.

CHAPER 49
ON THE BLOWER

Jaycee was at the front of fiona's home early that afternoon the time was nearing 1.30pm he stood by the side of his car parked up in the front of her driveway now fully clothed wearing a thick grey winter jumper,he had just popped out the house to get something from his car,he was about to open the door fiona called him

your mobile phone is ringing she shouted

okay he said not bothering to go into the car but turned around walking straight back into the house then into her living room where he had been moments ago sitting right besdie her after getting dressed upstairs in her bedroom after taking a hot shower washing away all the body sweat with scent of love making from himself after she had finished using the bathroom having a hot bath before him,he walked into the living room seeing her sitting there on the sofa with his mobile phone in her hand

she handed it to him saying the caller is birdy

ok babes thanks jaycee said

alright birdy whats up?jaycee asked slowly turning around from fiona walking back towards the front door walking once again to his car while talking on the phnoe

alright no problem,jaycee said on the phone before he finished talking putting his mobile in his black trouser pocket then opened his car driver side door,he collect the stuff from the car locked it back before going back into fiona's home.

CHAPTER 50

AT ALEX'S

Back at Alex flat stephen had just finished talking with jaycee on his mobile phone jaycee said he will be around in 1 hour maxium he said sitting on the sofa in the living room the two airbed which were on the floor earlier had now been deflatted then put away in the cupboard in the small hallway along with the pillows sheets and blankets.

Mark sat there next to his brother stephen on the sofa carl sat on the end next to him they had both woken up being in the living room about an hour now both eating up their breakfast with their plate on their laps while sitting there listening to everyone talking away,alex stood there in the gap between the kitchen and living room were there was suppose to be a kitchen door there he was standing in his spot when stephen said to him after speaking to jaycee that jaycee would be 1 hour

okay brother alex said standing there look toward his brother who had not so long finished washing himself in the bathroom putting on his jeans over his tracksuit bottom he had on secretively under his jeans all day yesterday and a clean fresh black t-shirt on Carlos sat on the armchair further down in the room nearest to the living room window he had also just finished his morning wash and had changed his clothing putting all his old clothes of yesterday with his night sleeping clothes into his sports bag which he had now placed in the hallway near to his sports trainers,he was sitting there listening to all what was being said in the living room while sipping on a nice hot cup of coffee having eaten up a late breakfast himself made by alex who had also made breakfast for all who needed it.

luis sat there on the armchair near the coffee table on the left side of the living room near to the kitchen entrance across from the sofa mark and carl also sat on

who wants a fag he said,picking up his half filled packet of cigarettes from the coffe table slipping one in his mouth then lighting it up with a red plastic lighter in his hand,feeling a lot better now from the earlier vomitting he had been heaving up from his guts this morning he felt a little relieved to be freed from the moments of terror torture with physical punishments which had taken hold of him earlier he was stuck in that toilet for over 20 minutes constantly vomitting wondering to himself when it was going to stop he hadn't felt so terrible in all his days this was he believed the worst of all drinking morning he had ever gone through,those bloody drinks he thought while he was bent over the toilet waiting for the next load of vomit to start pouring itself out from his mouth they are posionous and very dangerous he even started worrying thinking about blue flashing siren lights while he knelt there by the toilet thinking while wondering if he had given himself alcoholic posioning his mind now filled with uncertainty and doubts then he heard the bathroom door knocking

then stephen's voice asking him if he was okay,

he knew he weren't he felt really terrible wishing at that moment for this mornings nightmare to be over really wishing right there next to the toilet filled now with vomit just to be feeling normal i'm okay he told stephen

hearing stephen say okay,before outside in the hallway felt silent once again

then the vomiting time came upon him again while his mouth stank of the taste of vile alcohol his mouth was dry his tongue was dry,he was dyhydrated

he even thought right there about filling his mouth and body with toilet tap water then considered not to he was there on his knee for another 15 minutes before carlos came to the bathroom door calling his name

i'm okay he told carlos,I will be out soon

okay carlos said before telling him there's a couple of tablets on the living room's coffee table waiting for him with a glass of water

carlos then walked back into the living room to take the air out of his airbed and sort his stuff out while stephen laid there on the sofa.

luis left the toilet a few minutes later struggling to stand up straight entering the living room seeing stephen just behind his friend carlos opening up the curtains allowing the daylights to come into the living room,luis walked back to his airbed just feets infront of him laying down on it,

there's a glass of water and tablet there for you carlos said again on the table getting up walking over to the table with the packet of tablets and picked them up[

here you are luis,he said handing the water standing by the airbed he popped two tablets out of one of the strips in the packet here take these two he said handing them to luis

I feel terrible,he said taking the tablets from carlos

while stephen stepped away from the newly opened curtains watching carlos standing over luis handing him the glass of water luis put the two tablets in his mouth then drunk a little of the water swallowing the tablets then drunk the remainder of the water before handing the the glass back to carlos who stood there watching him.

I will take that stephen said walking to carlos

okay carlos said giving the glass to him,stephen then walked straight into the kitchen putting the empty glass in the kitchen sink.

luis laid there on the airbed for a little while his vomitting had stopped the fresh air coming in from the opened window uplifted his mood and feelings a lot as the activities of the late morning operated infront and beside also behind him as all those in the flat started waking up one by one entering the living room seeing luis laying there while stephen made himself something to eat for breakfast offering luis something to eat,luis refused saying he couldn't eat anything right now as stephen was putting his breakfast together carlos sat in the far seat near the window talking with luis when alex walked into the living room then around 10 minutes later mark came in then carl minutes after him Alex offered to fry up some late breaklfast for mark carl and luis then made up his mind to attempt to eat some now feeling a lot better more and more normal feeling stronger as the minutes moved along

after everyone had eaten also taken their turn in the bathroom for their wash luis was the last to get up feeling back to normal letting the air out from his airbed alex placed all the bedroom items with the airbed back into the hallway cupboard while luis used the bathroom getting his self changed putting his old clothes with night clothes into his rucksack then left it in the hallway next to carlos bag before taking his seat in the armchair next to the coffe table placing his packet of cigarettes and lighter on the table then laid back in the armchair listening to stephen talking on his mobile phone to one of his friends, before he finished talking,then put his phone onto his lap saying to alex,jaycee said about 1 hour

luis didn;t know what stephen meant but alex's knew because the both of them had been talking between each other while luis and carlos where talking in the living room,

stephen was talking to alex about thinking of asking Jaycee if he was interested in driving up to wales today to accompanying him with his brothers in visiting their sister's in Port Talbot and Swansea

stephen said he would call jaycee seeing if he was interested as alex stood inbetween the gap between the kitchen and the living room their younger brother mark sat beside stephen listening between the conversation while carl sat beside mark quiet as a mouse.

Stephen called jaycee' spoke with him,jaycee told him no problem he wouldn't mind taking a quick journey up to wales for he had never been there before and it would be a nice experience for him,

okay I will be at your brothers flat in a hour max he told stephen before they ended the conversation,that's when stephen told his brother alex that jaycee would be ringing on his buzzer in a hour.

will there be room in his car for me and carl,mark asked curiously

yeah there will be if you want to come

yeah okay mark and carl said

luis then asked them where they all were intending to go later ?

stephen already hearing luis and carlos speaking with each other about soon getting themslelves ready to make the journey back to london counted them out of making the journey to Wales with them we are all going to wales to visit my two sisters when jaycee comes in a hour,what you guys interested in following us,he asked luis

luis was still feeling a little mentally exhausted not feeling exactly 100% physically while he sat there in the armchair smoking his cigarette he had just lighten up after offering them around,

luis looked at carlos in the far corner sitting on the other arm-chair

what do you reckon ? luis asked him

well it depends how long you lot are going there fo, he asked stephen

while alex stood the in the gap of his kitchen listening on,so to did Mark and carl who both were smoking cigarettes with a ashtray on the end of the sofa they sat on near to carl

we are only going there for one night we will probably be back in bristol tomorrow evening it's just a sunday afternoon drive out to check my sisiters out

you two can come if you want your welcomed,stephen said as alex walked toward the door of the living room opened it then walkred on through the hallway to his bedroom to get himself changed ready for the journey to wales.

CHAPTER 51 COUNTRY AND CITY LIFE

Living life in the country side

living life in the country side towns

you will find trust in the people it's more stronger there

plenty of friendly faces

you will pass as you daily walk all around.

The crime rate is much lower

than in the big busy cities all over the lands

criminal activities still do always daily happen

there's always a jack the lad in every country town.

The community spirit seem much stronger

neighbours don't act like strangers to their neighbours

you will always see little children

always out happily playing

for in the countryside their lives feel less in dangers.

The city life with the country life

there is a big difference inbetween

even though they both share

the same prime minister kings with queens

Salty sea air when the breeze blows

peddle beaches sandy beaches with sand dunes

in the summer times these are the favourite places

where all the country people love to adventure

so then with mother nature they will always be in tune.

Little hills with high mountains

green open fields with farm yards

the smell of horse manure

to the farmers nose it doesn't smell that bad.

Bulls cows goats with sheeps

grazing in the meadows with green fields

dragon flies with butterflies

frogs toads nutes also tadpoles you will always see.

CHAPETR 52   ON THE MOVE

Both cars speed on along the A48 in the fast lane carlos had his foot down hard on the gas peddle trying his best to to keep up with Jaycee who had overtaken him just after they crossed the seven bridge passing the welcome to Wales sign,since then he had been following behind him most of the time at high speed,

this guy doesn't know how to cruise,carlos thought holding onto his steering wheel firmly keeping his focus on the white car infront of him trying not to allow a to large a gap to start forming,starting then to see himself trailing to far behind,he knew he was a little fortunate there were other cars up ahead which had slown jaycee down having him wait for them to move into the slower lane allowing him then to pass giving carlos that little bit of time to close the increasing gap but once there was a clear road infront of Jaycee he would quickly take advantage of this pushing is foot down while knocking up the gears moving faster ahead speedily while looking in his rearview mirror at carlos car slipping behind further back

stephen sat beside him in the passenger seat his seat belt fixed secure around him while alex sat alone in the back seat.

In carlos car luis sat in the passenger seat mark and sat in the back seats carlos had his music system on playing the tunes of the artist *TLC* while they all sat there listening to the music of *No Scrubs* in the afternoon lights which would soon be growing darker outside of the car the weather was far away from brilliant even though the roads were surprisingly dry for this time of the year for no rains fell today but the temperature was on a low not far from minus degre the coldness of the outside air could clearly be felt if you were not wearing your thick winter jacket today.

luis his hangover had completelty vanished once again he was back to feeling normal even reminding himself he would never wish to revisit that mental and physical alcoholic pathway ever again also to be more careful when it comes to strong drinks which was to always avoid mixing your drinks if anything just stick to the same brand of drinks all night,then you would have less things to worry about the next morning,he sat there in the passenger seat watching carlos struggling to keep up to the speed of jaycee while listening to the music playing aeway in the car

his minds memories started to drift back to the days when he was in the prison system with mark who was now just sitting in the car behind him his mind taking him right back to the moment when leroy said he was going to teach francis a lesson and he would revenge luis by doing the job for leroy saying he had nothing to lose but mark had a lot more to lose like his prison time,leroy and luis knowing mark was now on the last part of his sentence and would be released in a few months

when my path crossed with francis I will straighten him out making him know what is what he was telling the both of them that evening in thre large tv room and I don't even need a plan he told them as he sat there

that evening went by with no contact between leroy and francis

the next day on the prison wing leroy left his cell on the landing,he didn't have a cell mate but was waiting to hear what the answer to the question was after his cousin mark asked the prison warden later today if he could be doubled up sharing a cell with leroy, right now mark was not sharing a cell with a inmate

luis was also on his own with no cell mate,

leroy walked down the landing to the ground floor to collect his breakfast this morning he knew he wouldn't be seeing francis also if he did he couldn't do anything to him because he was not on the same landing as him francis was on the 1st landing while leroy was on landing no.3,there was a prison order when it came to meal times breakfast dinner with evening meals this was the prison officer would always only let one landing out of their cells to go down the ironstairs to the ground floor at a time they would either unlock all the cell doors on the 1st landing sending them down to get their meals then they would lock each prisoner's cell doors back up one at a time until the last one on that landing was locked away,then they would start to unlock all the cells on landing number 2 doing exactly the same thing then landing number 3 sometime they would unlocking landing number 3 first then then work their way down,it all depended on how they felt.

today this morning they started unlocking landing 3 first when leroys cell was unlocked he grabbed his blue plastic cup then walked on the landing in his blue prison jeans and blue t-shirt joined on with the few other convicts on the landing walked on down the ironstairs hearing other cell doors on his landing unlocking he was hungry he couldn't wait for his breakfast so he could fill his stomach,he got his silver steel tray from the pick up point had his breakfast served onto his tray by the inmates who's job it was to serve the meals as all the morning screws looked on he then filled his big plastic cup with hot water then walked on back up the ironstairs to his landing then into his cell using one of his feet to pull the slightly opened cell fully open while holding onto his tray of breakfast and tea he walked into his cell then back kick the cell door shut before taking a seat on his iron bed with the steel tray now on his lap,the tv was on in his cell on a small old looking wooden table just above the table you could see a small white wooden framed window which were closed tight behind them you would see when opened up black painted iron bars.

he sat there eating his breakfast looking at the tv screen the morning news was on the tv the news presenter speaking about the new prime minister and what his intentions were to do about brexit,leroy put the silver tray on the floor by his feet got up turning the tv channel over to another channel then went straight back to his iron bed climbing on to it

mm,his belly felt okay now no more hungry feelings he thought laying down on top of the green netted blanket francis came to his mind while a smile appeared on his face francis two other friends also came to his mind one of them two of them or three of them he thought laying there,should he beat them up one at a time or just beat one of them up to spread the warning this morning he laid there contemplating on his iron bed with his big round eyes staring up at the much needed old looking white painted ceiling

even though leroy had not that long ago been let out of the segragation block being kept down in the isolation depart- ment for over 3 months separated from all the convicts losing all the priviledges he was glad to be back on the wing with all the other inmates having only been back a few days before luis was transfered to this prison only days before his cousin Mark arrived.

now he was definetly up for a bit of fun,he didn't really care how things would end up as long as he didn't end up oin the hospital ward of the prison or lost his life then everything else below these two things were very minor to him,he knew he couldn't lose prison days on his sentence because he still didn't have an EDR date also every parole date which came his way throughout the years he had spent in the prison system he had now been refused so right now he was even more pissed off with the prison system right now he didn't really give a damn and who ever stood in his way was now certain to feel his anger.

right now he was waiting on two thing at this moment in the prison

the first was waiting to see what job the prison officers were going to give to him which he had been waiting on since being brought back to the wing secondly he was waiting for his cousin to let him know if the prison officer will be moving him to his cell to be his cell mate he laid there with his head filled up with thoughts with the tv on having nothing to do but either fall back asleep or think on.

He feel asleep not even realising it until he was awoken by the sound of steel keys a going into a steel lock on his steel cell door his cell door was pushed opened as he turned around on his iron bed getting up looking towards his cell door at the prison officer standing in his cell by the cell door in his white long sleeved shirt with black trousers on.

leroy sat on his iron bed looking at him, then called out his name Douglas with his prison number,we got some work for you to start get yourself up and put on your shoes and follow me he said standing there with a clip board in his hand,leroy got up put on his shoes saying to the officer

what kind of work is it officer,now grabbing his grey jumper from the wooden cupboard next to his tv putting it on over his head pulling it down over his body as his two arms found the they need to be pulled through so he could see his two hands as his head popped out from the top of his juimper to hear the prison officer say your working in the laundry lad a nice warm job for you in this cold weather leroy smiled walked over to the prison officer who had made enough room for him to walk straight pass him on through his cell door as the prison officer stepped out of the cell after him shut your cell door then lad,he said stepping to one side on the landing not to far from his cell door watching leroy slam shut the cell door then followed the officer down the landing down the ironstairs to the ground floor onwards to the laundry department the prison officer took him into the laundry leaving him there with the laundry manager to show him all the duties he will have to be doing daily while he worked there.

as he was being shown his duties there were atleast twenty other prison inmates in the laundry department some stuffing hand full of clothes into big large washing machines some taking clothes out of big huge dryers while other clothes dryers were spinning around the laundry was a very busy noisey place and very humid everyone in there was busy fully occupied as leroy was being walked around being shown what each machinery was to be used for as he slowly walked floor of the laundry with the manager

his eyes came across spotting one of francis friends who was to busy to notice him okay leroy thought it certainly is his lucky day today as he continued on listening to the manager

ok Douglas come into my office he said leroy followed him,

now all prison officer on the landing with people who worked in the prison system would only call all inmated by their surnames,leroy took a seat in the managers office as the manager asked his full name with his prison number so he could put his name on his work sheet then told him to follow him back onto the laundry floor taking him to one of the inmates who was the supervisor over all the other prison workers he was the one to show leroy what job he had to do the manager left this inmate to it,a very short time later every one was told to stop work and get themselves ready to go back to their cells when the prison officers came for it was now dinner time

leroy stood there talking with the inmate in charge until two prison officers came to escort all the mates back to the wing and bang them all up until their landings one at a time would be unlocked for dinner.

leroy sat on his iron bed while he waited for his cell to be unlocked for dinner time his blood was running he could not believe all what had happened in the last 1 hour getting a new job in the laundry then his surprise spotting one of francis friends who worked in there the thoughts made him get up from off his iron bed onto his feet placing his two hands over his mouth like he was trying his best to muzzle the laughter that had just jumped out from his mouth he was hyped up like a hungry dog who hadn't been fed for days now being fully starved but had just stumbled on a big large piece of chunky fresh delicious sweet meat there was only one direction his mind was now focused on and this was to beat the living day lights out of francis friend asap if not beat him to the pulp well atleast somehow draw a little bit of his blood maybe a thick lip he thought climbing back onto his iron bed with his mind thinking on overtime a missing tooth or two maybe I could break his nose if I hit him in the right place hard enough I done that a few times before he smiled sitting there thinking of the image of francis with one big black eye then two black eyes a broken jaw,many images started flowing through his mind as he waited for his cell door to be unlocked.

CHAPTER 53   ON THE GO

Jaycee just pass the sign on the A48 which said Port Talbot the next turning off a couple hundred yards on the left,he looked into his rearview mirror once again,carlos his car could not be seen he was nowhere in sight the few cars a little behind him was not his car

take the next left,birdy said,

looking to his right at jaycee,who's eyes just came off looking through his rear view mirror,focusing on the road ahead of him,

I know I just pass the sign,he said,just direct me once i've turned of the motorway he told birdy,then he flicked his left indicator light on,driving safetly into the left lane driving onto the left skip road which took him into Port Talbot town,

now stephen hadn't been back into his old town for a while as Jaycee drove on into the slip road then entered a big round-about which stephen knew, from then onwards the next road would take you straight through onto the town centre but all the roads had now changed

stephen realised after jaycee had passsed the big roundabout

bloody heck,I haven't seen this road before,he said,trying to direct jaycee onto the right direction

don't worry he said,take that turning instead,

then a little further along he came across another new road a new route saying hold on a moment jaycee,

while stephen started seeing,getting a little confused with the new roads leading to the town centre from Margam,

they have built up so many new roads with new routes all the normal roads have disappeared he said to Jaycee,trying his best now to use a little bit of common sense to direct his driver so they both didn,t get lost in the town he had grown up in

it was not yet dark they both could easily see the roads infront of them but stephen thought to himself the old town he had grown up in now looked more like a brandnew town,he kept directing jaycee until he knew exactly where he was,he was now finally in the area where his older sister lucy lived.

CHAPTER 54
A LITTLE BEHIND

Just a few minutes behind on the A48 Carlos came to the slip road which took them pass the big roundabout in to Port Talbot with mark and carl sitting at the back of the car showing them the direction's to lucy's home' carlos had turned the volume of the music system down on a low level so he could hear the direction's from Mark and sometimes carl directing him through the town

luis had broken off from thinking of the prison memory days of being saved by mark and leroy,his mind was back in the reality times of the present

wales he thought,looking towards his left at many high huge green hills which could even been call little mountains which rose up to the heights of around 800 feet tall,situated right by the side of the A48 motorway on the side of Port Talbot town

Have you ever been up there ? he pointed at the mountain looking hills asking mark and carl,

they both looked at luis from the back seat

carl said yeah man

mark said of course plenty of times

carlos drove on while saying'

what there's only sheeps you will find up there iv'e been told on the welsh mountains,then he laughed

luis joined in with the laughter

there's not just sheeps up there answered carl

while not fully understanding the joke

there's plenty of magic mushrooms as well

magic mushrooms luis said,looking around at carl and mark

seeing mark smiling back at him,then nodding his head,saying yes plenty of magic mushroom starts growing on top of those mountains in certain fields, this time of year,they start growing in autumn,we are nearly coming to the end of the season,now they will soon be disappearing until next year autumn

Oh you hear what they are saying carlos ?luis said turning around looking at him

while carl told carlos you need to take that right turning at the end of the road

I heard them luis,it sounds very interesting he said as he drove on following carl's instructions

take the next left mark then said,carlos did so

Just park up anywhere near here,mark then said

carlos slowed down his car then found a parking space in the street

there's jaycee's car,mark said pointing across the road on the right a few cars down from where they had stopped,

jaycee's car was parked up right opposite of lucy's home

there was no one in his car

alright you coming in boys,mark said opening the back door climbing out then he stood by the side of the car as carl opened his side of the car got out onto the quiet road in the street shutting the door walking around the back end of the car then stood beside mark

they both waited for luis and carlos to come out of the car carlos then locked his car him and luis followed mark and carl to lucy's front door.

CHAPTER 55 AT LUCY'S

Just a few hours early that afternoon around 12.40pm lucy's front door to her home was knocking,she knew exactly who would be standing at the front door because she was expecting,a visit,she was in the dining room when the door started to knock,she got up from one of the four varnished wooden chairs which surrounded the table she sat at,her eyes quickly glimpsed the clock hanging on the dining room wall near the table showing the time 12.40pm

Mm she's on time,well 5 minutes early,she told herself as she walked pass the front room her husband Vernon was in laying on the sofa watching the tv

didn't you hear the door knocking? she said looking at him laying there

Yes lucy,was his only reply

She continued on through the small hallway,opened up her front door

Hi jean,come in she said

alright lucy,her younger sister replied,who had just drove from swansea city to visit her this Sunday afternoon

jean was two years younger than lucy and 11 months 3 weeks just under 1 year older than her brother stephen

Jean and stephen shared the same age each and every year for 19 days then it was jeans birthday in december once again she would be that 1 year older than her brother stephen again.

lucy and jean stayed in the dining room chatting away at the table while vernon laid there on the front room sofa relaxed watching the tv programmes then they both went out into the kitchen at the back of the home to peel and cut up some vegetables,skin the fresh chicken,dicing it into small pieces and boil some rice

it was about 25 minutes later the front door started to knock

lucy and jean didn't hear the knocking

this time vernon got up from the sofa walked out into the hall-way opening the front door

Oh hello alex,he said looking very surprised to see his brother in law standing infront of him

Oh he said again,seeing stephen climbing out the passenger seat of a white car,parked right across the road

who's that with him ? he asked alex

It's a friend of stephen from london his nasme is jaycee

where's my sister ? he added,walking pass Vernon

who made space for him moving a little to the hallways right wall

She's in the kitchen I think alex,he replied

Ok you go see the others in,alex said,

before walking off passed the front room into the dining room

as stephen and jaycee got to the front door

while the car was nicely parked and locked up properly.

◆ ◆ ◆

CHAPTER 56   AT BIG SISTER'S

Everyone was now in the living room,lucy had turned the cooker down onto a low number allowing the food to simmer while the rice pot was turned compleltely off,she sat at the dining room table,vernon sat beside her on one of the chairs on the three sofa's in the dining room,one was directly facing the dining rooms table lucy vernon jean also stephen sat at where alex sat on the one while jaycee sat on the one a little further back in the room near the kitchen.

    Jaycee was introduced to everyone,stephen told his sisters mark would soon be knocking on the front door with carl and two Portuguese coming down from London,it was less than 10 minutes before the front door started to knock again,lucy left her seat at the table walking out of the room in through the hallway to the front door,as it knocked again she opened it

    Hi sis mark,said,standing there with a big smile exposed on his face

carl luis and carlos were all standing behind him

Hi young mark,she said to her youngest brother the youngest of the bird family

I got some friends with me okay,he said,looking at his oldest sister the oldest child of the bird children belonging to Stanford Bird and Birdie Bird who came from the carribean island in jamaica to great britain in the year 1957 before jamaica was made indepent getting their indepence in 1961

Yes come in mark and you guys,she said smiling at them all before she stepped to the right side of the hallway giving mark enough space to walk in through her front door into the hall-way with the others

go into the dining room mark,she said

he passed her the three others walked in all saying hello to her as they passed her to follow mark into the dining room before lucy closed her front .

CHAPTER 57   AT SIS HOME

Everyone was now together in lucy's home,lucy being surprise to see her home filled with unexcpected guests today this sunday because she was only expecting a visit from her sister jean but now here home was very busy,what a nice lovely sunday she thought,while she had been sitting back on her chair at the table looking around her living room at everyone talking and laughing away,the atmosphere was warm very friendly,the food in the kitchen had finished being cooked she dished out a plate of chicken and rice with vegetables to anyone who wanted a plate full helped by jean

everyone had a plate herself and jean were surprised they had cooked just the right amount for everyone to get a decent size plate of a nice hot Sunday meal.

now a little time had passed since mark had arrived with the others.

At the back of the house mark and luis was they were standing in the small square shaped concrete paved stone garden with carlos,all smoking a cigarette for lucy wouldn't allow any smoking in her home,she and her husband were non smokers.

Lucy still sat there at the dining room table with her husband and jean after they had taken all the empty plates from the dining room leaving them in the kitchen sink to be washed up later,there they sat stephen's place at the table was empty for he had only a few minutes ago left the home with jaycee they were going to a small off licence shop which was just a 2 minute walk away from lucy's home,stephen wanted to buy a few alcoholic drinks,Jaycee needed to buy a packet of cigarettes having only one left in his packet.

Alex sat on the sofa not to far away from the dinnig room table carl sitting next to him all those on the table with alex and carl were talking among each other.

Stephen and jaycee stood at the shop counter,Jaycee had bought his cigarettes while stephen was taking out a £20 note from his wallet to pay for a bottle of wrey and nephew's white rum when he felt a hand tap him on the back of his shoulder then a voice said alright stephen,he looked around as Jaycee stood there looking now at the stranges face who had tapped stephen on his shoulder

Hay alright dennis how are you ?

stephen said seeing who it was

then he said alright winston long time don't see

dennis was a cousin of stephen his 1st cousin

dennis his dad luther and stephens dad stanford who both came from jamaica were half brothers

dennis was 1 year older than stephen

winston who came into the shop with dennis was an older person

he was dennis uncle who stephen used to live with in the south of london in an area called newcross in the year 2003 for about 6 month

winston was now down in port talbot visiting family

alright dennis and winston let me pay for this then I will talk to you guys

he turned back to the counter giving the cashier £20 took his change

I will wait here,he said to them both,pointing to the shop entrance door.

At the same time in the back yard at lucy's home luis was asking mark all kinds of questions about the magic mushrooms that was made mention of earlier in the car

Yeah he told luis standing there smoking the cigarette while carlos stood next to luis listening to what mark was saying

yeah the guys in this town pick them every year in augusat to november on the mountains

can we go and pick some tomorrow ? luis asked,standing there with his back against the outside kitchen wall in the early dark evening also smoking while he listened in interest about the magic mushrooms growing freely up in the mountains of this country town in the country of wales where he and his friend had never been in their lives,he had heard about magic mushrooms liked most people he knew in london who had heard of them but had never tried them.

I wouldn't mind experiencing what people would call a trip,he thought while listening to what mark had to say,

mark telling luis, he hadn't had a trip for years,the last time was in his teen years

alright me and carl will take you guys up to the fields in the mountains where we know some of them do defineltly grow okay,

luis and carlos said yes bruv,thats cool standing there before them.

There were many fields up in the mountains of port talbot in the high hills some would call them which couldn't be ignored for they ran all the way along the right hand side of the entry into the small town right through to the other end of the town continuing on the 48 motorway running along side just below the giant hills which were about 850 feet in height,a person could be up in the green hills searching through the many fields all over the the hills for magic mushrooms and could easily come up empty handed for there were only certain fields up there where you would find them growing wildly in their thousands and tens of thousands scattered in their bundles here there and everywhere in the clusters and bunches of twenties here forty there in their little patches which they grew in,pulling them up from out off the earth one at a time then bagging them up small long thinned stems with a small umberalla shaped looking mushroom head at the top some coloured in white or grey sometimes their tops would become dark brown if the rains were falling.

Back outside the off licence just a few minutes away from lucy's home stephen was outside standing just a few feet away from the shop door entrance talking with his cousin dennis and dennis uncle winston,

jaycee stood by stephen side he had opened his packet of cigarettes which had only one left inside while Stephen spoke on to dennis

jaycee was smoking his cigarette the new packet he had bought was now in his trousers front pocket while the old packet he had put into a bin which was outside just by the side of the off licence shop.

dennis was telling stephen he should pass around by Jimmy,s nightclub on Station Road the main road in the town in the town centre where an old black man a good friend of the bird family owned a night club it was were most of the blacks of the town went for a drink

yes I will be going there tonight winston said to stephen as he was untying his two dog leads of the big rottweillers which was tied to a drain pipe outside the shop connected to the shops wall.

Yes stephen come you must come and show your face birdman,he said then laughed,birdman,he said again,reminding stephen this was always how he use to address him in the days when stephen use to stay at his flat with him

And bring your friends winston said standing with the dogs leads now held tightly in his one hand

okay I may see you tonight then okay guys,Stephen replied

jaycee hailed the both of them saying okay guys just before dennis and his uncles walk off in a different direction to where stephen and jaycee were to walk back to.

CHAPTER 58   OUT
ON THE ROAD

The time clock of the early evening had now moved itself forward a little now in port talbot town,walking up Station Road the mainstreet of the town was Stephen alex mark jaycee luis and carlos the six of them all heading to Jimmy's Bar,jaycee had left his car parked in the same spot in lucy's street so to did carlos,everyone of them were feeling merry hearted right now after drinking a good amount of white rum between them at lucy's home when stephen come back from the off licence earlier with jaycee with a big bottle of wray and nephew rum,the name of the drink a well known rum in the carribean island of jamaica for it's powerful strength,he did ask lucy who was sitting at the table as soon as he got back to give him some drinking glasses,she got up went into a cupboard in the dining room in the far corner opposite the dining rooms entry door near the hallway it was in there she kept her drinking glasses for alcohol drinks,

jaycee took his seat back in the sofa near to the kitchen wall passing alex and carl who were still sitting talking with jean and vernon everyone was busy chatting away when stephen and jaycee got back mark,luis and carlos were still outside in the back garden

ucy asked stephen once she had got to her drinking cabinet if he could go into the kitchen and get her a plastic tray,

you will see a few of them on the kitchen unit near the sink,she told him no problem stephen said before placing the bottle of rum with a bottle of coke onto the table right in the centre of the dining table,then said with a cheeky grin to jean and vernon don't touch that now okay,then walked off into the kitchen coming back with a red gold and green plastic tray walking straight in-between the sofa alex and carl were,

on and the dining room table jean and vernon sat by

stephen walked over to lucy who was holding two glasses in her hand ready to place them on to the tray,Sstephen held onto the tray while lucy filled the tray with various shapes of drinking glasses

You can take them into the kitchen and I will give them a quick wash she said closing the door for the cabinet then followed stephen to the kitchen as he was walkling towards jaycee sitting a little ahead of him Jaycee said I'm going to go back to that off licence and grab another bottle of that white rum so we can all have a good drink I'm not going to be driving anywhere tonight if your going out to the bar

okay stephen told him,give me a minute I will follow you before he walked into the kitchen with the tray of glass in his hand,lucy right behind him watching him putting them onto the unit,he looked toward his left where the kitchen back door was slightly opened,he could see through the kitchen window mark out there talking with someone,he assumed it would be either luis or carlos then looked back at lucy before passing her,he said I will be back now,oh can you just put the clean glasses next to the bottle of rum on the table sis

okay she said,turning on the hot water tap

the next thing Stephen was gone

stephen and jaycee went back to the off licence buying a bottle of wray and nephew with a bottle of coke then made their way back to the house opening the rum filling drinking glasses mixed with the coke,handing everyone a glass each,the two bottles of rum were completely finished by the time everyone who wanted to go out to Jimmy bars was ready

the time was getting on

jean had only a little sip of the white rum not even enough to make her even merry for she knew she had to drive the 9 miles back home to Swansea city,she left lucy's home the same time the six of the lads who were now walking up station road had left.

vernon her husband stayed at home with his wife lucy who didn't drink any of the white rum,she only drank a bit of the coke

carl left telling mark he was going to go back to his place of home which was in the sandfields estate area of the town

We will see you later lucy,okay her brothers said before they started the walk towards the town centre with jaycee luis and carlos now they were all feeling tipsy walkling towards the entrance of jimmy's bar passing a few wine bars still opened on station road with a few people walking up and down coming out from the wine bars or entering in them,the two busiest nights of the town had already passed friday and saturday nights sunday night on the main street of station road was usually like a week day night very quiet with only a few people to be seen as it was to be expected even though you could hear the music playing from inside Jimmy's bar when they all walked in through the entrance door they only found a hand full of people in there,two of them were dennis and winston.

CHAPTER 59
ANOTHER DAY

Another night had been fully spent another Sunday was now completely over,a new morning had started a brandnew day had already arrived coming with the wet falling early winter rains,lightly falling to the grounds wetting up the roads with streets all over the south of wales .

Back at lucy's home lucy sat on her bed in her bedroom sipping on a nice lovely hot cup of morning tea,she had just climbed back up the staircase to her bedroom after making the tea in the kitchen,quietly walking passed jaycee sleeping on the dining room sofa

while stephen was fast asleep on the other one,they were both given light sheets to cover with last night by lucy,the dining room was comfortably warm they both came in with alex luis carlos and mark just passed the hours of 2.30 am all of them staying at jimmys bar until it closed at 2am then walked back through the streets of the town back to lucy's home where they stayed in the living room with lucy and vernon chatting away until the late hour when the tiredness of sleep caught up with them all,they were all crashed out sleeping like babies before the clock arrived at 4pm lucy giving stephen and Jaycee a light sheet to cover with before leaving them to sleep off the alcohol effects before she retired for the night upstairs in her bedroom leaving alex asleep on the settee in the front room downstairs

while upstairs in the back small bedroom mark was in there

asleep on his own,luis and carlos shared the front bedroom on the left next door to lucy and vernons bedroom in there luis and carlos slept head to toe back to back.

lucy was first up the next morning only getting a few hours of sleep but she weren't tired she just felt the need for a hot drink,it was how she ended up downstairs walking then passing jaycee and stephen before going back upstairs.

now she sat on her bed sipping on her tea her husband was asleep in the bed the tv in the bedroom was on with the volume on a very low level where you could just about hear what the people was showning on the tv screen talking about

all around the rest of the home this morning it was peaceful very quiet everyone was fast asleep except herself,she will leave them all resting until they are ready to get up she told herself as her eyes looked at the tv set.

As the time moved onwards Jaycee started waking up from his sleep stretching his legs under the light sheet,rubbing his eyes with his one hand while laying there on his back,his eyes fully opened turning now over onto his side realising he was in his friends sister's home in her dining room

he could see stephen a few feet away sleeping on the sofa as jaycee laid there on his side letting out a low quiet sounding tired yawn,he didn't have a clue what the time was but something was telling him it weren't early in the morning even though there was no daylight to be seen from where he was laying the curtains in the room which were right behind him they were drawn closed the door to the kitchen just a few feet away passed his head to the left was also closed also the door to the dining room just passed the sofa Stephen was sleeping on to the left,this door was also closed,the room was neither dark neither light he could see all that was in the dining room but not clearly,it was the curtains light behind him which lighted up the room a little bit with the slight daylights squeezing through at its end, jaycee had put his trouser and jumper last night after lucy had left the room he left his shoes in the hallway on the floor,leaning up on the sofa then bending over toward the end of the sofa reaching over picking up his trousers in his hand bringing it forward to his chest he started searching his pockets for his mobile phone,the light sheet was now only covering him from his waist down to his feet his mobile was on but placed on silent mode,laying himself back down looking at it laying there on his back Jaycee not realising neither noticing there was a clock on the dining room wall,he could see he had 2 miss call showing on his mobile phone checking,seeing one of them was fiona had been trying to call him early in the morning with a text message she left asking him his he back home in london yet

he laid there smiling while thinking to himself london it seemed a million miles away from being in this room in this house in this little country town called port talbot.

Yesterday when he first sat down in the sofa he was now laying on he was admiring all the bob marley framed pictures which were hung up on the wall in the room big ones with small ones with a lot of other rasta coloured pictures of lions inside frames also noticing a large framed picture of michael jackson doing his moonwalk motion,there were so many pictures he had thought with so many different types of ornaments,he noticed they were not just in the dining room but every room he had been into in lucy's home

Mm,interesting he thought to himself yesterday

He held onto his trousers and his mobile getting up from the sofa,stood up slipped his trousers on then walked pass stephen quietly opening the dining rooms door picked his black sports trainers up in the hallway then went back into the dining room closing the door walking passed stephen again as his hand felt through his trousers pocket feeling his packet of cigarettes while walking on into the kitchen seeing the key for the kitchen door was already in the doors keyhole,he turned the handle it was locked so he unlockerd the door opened it but didn't take a step out being put off by the falling rain so he stood there with the kitchen back door open taking a cigarette out from the packet his cigarette lighter was in the same pocket,he took it out lightening up his cigarette then put it back into his pocket taking a deep pull on the cigarette taking his mobile phone out from his pocket pressed his finger on a few digits while the cigarette hanged down from his lips then waited for the voice of Fiona to come onto his phone.

CHAPTER.60 AT LUCY'S

Around about the same time upstairs at lucy's home mark was walking on the landing feeling tired after just waking up he was on his way to used the bathroom which was just infront of him he walked to it closing the door behind him after a few minutes her had flushed the chain washed his hand and was now walking back to his bedroom on the landing to get a little bit more sleep,feeling he wasn't quite ready to get up yet not realising how late the time was,when the front bedroom door opened then luis stepped out

Oh he said looking seeing mark in his boxer shorts with vest on slowly walking bare footed on the landing towards his direction on the way back to his room

Your up before me he said,jokingly

nah not really mark replied tiredly,stopping infront of him,I just used the tolilet i'm going back to bed i'm knackered man

whats the time he asked luis,while he stood there right by the bedroom luis had walked out from,

I don't know it must be nearly afternoon know bruv luis stated then said hold on,turning around going back into the bedroom to check on the time on his mobile phone which he had put on a cabinet in the room

he picked it up looking at it saying,mm,to himself,when he saw what the time was,he was a little surprised putting his mobile phone back on the cabinet then walked back out of the bedroom finding mark had disappeared,

luis knew what bedroom mark was in quietly closing his door then walked the few steps to the bedroom mark was,giving the door a few knocks before inviting himself into the room without being asked,

mark was by the window his head inbetween the two curtains looking through the white netted curtains behind the curtains down into the back garden,

he could see it was raining,he could also see jaycee standing below him to the right where he could see the kitchen door open jaycee standing right by the opened door smoking a cigarette while talking to someone on his mobile phone

I thought I could hear someone talking,mark said turning around

Its jaycee,mark said looking at luis

So are we still going to be going up them mountains to pick some magic mushroom luis asked standing inside the bedroom with the door now closed,so he and mark could have a bit of private conversation while he stood there in his baggy boxer shorts which dropped down pass his knees with his t-shirt on

mark walked by his bed then sat on it looking at luis infront of him,

whats the time then he asked luis

I don't know,he said

well by the time we get dressed and eat then make our way to the mushroom fields it will be getting dark out there and you can't be picking mushrooms in the dark,

mark had to laughed,he couldn't help himself but to laugh at what he had just said,

luis stood there then smiled when mark laughed

fully understanding what mark was saying,he even knew why he laughed it also made luis smile even bigger even though he felt a bit disappointed because he wanted to pick some mushrooms today to take back to london with him

the weathers terrible mark stated as he sat there talking

we can go up the mountain early tomorrow morning if you want I will take you to the field

luis stood there for a moment silent,then said I don't know whether carlos is going back to london today once he gets up we were suppose to be back in the city yesterday evening to be honest with you bruv he said as he stood there by the door now starting to scratch the little stubble of hair he could feel on the side of his chin running the four fingers on his one hand down his face.

I will wake him up and ask him

ok luis,mark said now laying down on his bed

luis opened the bedroom door walking out closing it behind him.

CHAPTER 61
WAKING UP

Downstairs stephen had just opened his eyes been woken up by a voice coming from the kitchen,he quickly recognised turning his head towards the sofa jaycee was laying on seeing it was now empty,even though jaycee had closed the door in the dining room which lead onto the kitchen he still woke stephen by his loud talking,

stephen took the light sheet from off himself just wearing his boxers with t-shirt,he got up walking fairly tired towards the kitchen door opened it then walked into the kitchen

as jaycee who still stood by the opened kitchen door still talking away on his mobile looked at him giving him the thumbs up sign with his free hand

do you want a hot or cold drink ? stephen asked walking further into the kitchen toward the electric kettle

yeah I will have a cold drink,he said inbetwen his talking on the phone standing in the same spot as stephen started to fill up the kettle with cold water,on the kitchen unit there were a stack of clean glasses which were used yesterday evening but had not been put back into the dining rooms cabinet stephen turned around to the fridge behind him opened it to see what drinks were in there

jaycee finished talking on his mobile phone stepping back into the kitchen closing the door,the cigarette he was smoking had burnt itself out right down to the brown cork between his fingers while he held a packet of cigarettes in that same hand his mobile in his other hand

there's orange juice apple juice mango juice pine apple juice, stephen said

pour us some mango juice can you replied jaycee

yeah no problem,stephen replied taking the juice out from the fridge keeping the fridge door opened looking at Jaycee

you can put your cig end in the kitchen bin just pour a little tap water on it first okay

there's no ashtrays in this house as you have probably already noticed

let me pour you this juice first Stephen continued to say,walking back to the kitchen unit picking up a half pint glass from the load of drinking glasses then washed the glass giving it a swil out then poured mango juice into it filling it up,

jaycee standing there to the right side of him near the kitchen sink

stephen walked back to the fridge putting the mango juice back inside then closed the fridge door

jaycee was now damping the cig end under the water tap,then walked to the kitchen bin near the kitchen door pressed his foot on the bin pedal watching the lid open then dropped the wet cig end into it,taking his foot end off it allowing it to automatically close

while stephen got a cup from the kitchen cupboard near the fridge the kettle water had clicked off the water was boiled

it's your bristol girl you was talking to ah jaycee,stephen asked

getting a tea spoon from the draw near the kitchen sink

jaycee moved near the kitchen door which took you back into

the dining room holding the glass of mango juice in his hand taking a sip

then answered yeah,it's my bristol girl

haven't your girl in finchley called you yet,

he asked,standing there now taking another sip of the juice watching stephen spooning some sugar from out of the sugar bowl

yeah i've been in contact with her only by text messages though,I told her just to communicate by texts unless it's something really important stephen said,now taking out some coffee from out of the coffee jar with a different tea spoon

okay jaycee said,i'm in the dining room,okay he said then opened the kitchen door walking into the dining room leaving the door open

  While upstairs lucy had just opened her bedroom door to see what activities was going on due to sitting there on her bed hearing movements on the upstairs landing only a minute or so ago the landing was empty seconds later luis opened the door to the bedroom he had slept in next door to,lucys bedroom the bedroom mark was in was directly opposite to lucys bedroom

good morning lucy said to luis,lookings at him dressed only in his boxer shorts with t-shirt bare footed

hi good morning lucy,luis, said standing on the landing right outside his bedroom door

are you hungry,i'm about to do some breakfast for who ever wants to eat ?

yeah that would be nice luis answered

what about your friend does he want anything

I will ask him right now,luis answered turning quickly around opening the door

carlos do you want breakfast?,he asked

yes came the answer

okay luis said then closed back the bedroom door

yes he said looking towards lucy who was now about to nock on her younger brothers marks door

okay she replied to luis,then knocked on the door

luis stood just beside because he already needed to speak to mark letting him know that carlos would stay in port talbot for another day so he would have time to get some magic mushrooms up there in the high tall green hills which loooked like mountains to him

he waited there for lucy to finish talking to mark which was just a quick question

do you want some breakfast ?

yes was mark answer

lucy then stepped back out from marks room turning towards luis keeping the door open saying to luis,

that now was the oppurtunity for him to use the bathroom before coming down for breakfast for it was the only bathroom in the house.

lucy had been living in this house only 2 years since moving from the top end of town in a area called,Margam to this area called fairfield

okay luis said to her before she started making her way downstairs to the front room to see if alex was still sleeping or awake,she pushed the front room door open quietly

mm,he's still sleeping she said looking at her brother stretched out on the three seater sofa with a sheet covering him the front room curtains closed keeping out the morning lights,she walked into the room leaving the door slightly opened then called out alex's name

his eyes opened looking red from the sleep he had just broken

alright sis he said,whats up ?

lucy came right up to the sofa looking down at him laying there

i'm going into the kitchen,i'm starting to make some breakfast,do you want some breakfast ?

yes sis thats nice of you I will be up soon,okay

alright,she said,before going back through the front rooms door closing it while standing now in the small hallway

luis was now in the bedroom mark was in,happily telling him he will be glad to go to the magic mushroom patch with him tomorrow,he was now going to use the bathroom before going downstairs for breakfast.

When lucy entered the dining room stephen was sitting on one of the chairs at the dining rooms table drinking a cup of coffee Jaycee sat on another chair at the table near to him with a empty half pint glass infront of him on the table

good morning she said,as soon as she entered the room

stephen looked to his left so did jaycee

they both said good morning lucy

she asked the both of them if they also wanted breakfast,

they both said yes

okay she said walking pass the both of them counting now in her mind how many all together including herself was to have breakfast

she came to the figure 8 standing now in the middle of the kitchen .

Jaycee popped his head into the kitchen asking lucy if she had any clean towels he could use

yes there's plenty of them in the cupboard in the upstairs landing,she told him before he told stephen he was going upstairs for a quick wash and get changed,

as he got to the bathroom he found it was already in use

hay who's in the bathroom ?he said with a loud joking humourus voice

it's me luis

are you going to be long in there,Jaycee asked,looking to the right a few yards to him on the landing seeing the cupboard lucy was telling him about where she kept her towels

no i'm nearly done just another minute,luis shouted from the bathroom

okay,jaycee answered,holding his trousers in one hand walking over to the cupboard opening it seeing a load of towels of different colours stacked up on one of the shelves with light sheets of differet colours on the other shelf he took out a towel then closed the cupboard door.

downstairs alex was up out of the sofa folding up the light sheet which had covered him leaving it on the arm of the sofa,his trousers he had left at the end of the sofa side further in the room,he picked them up then put them on,he left the room leaving the door ajar walking a few steps through the hallway in through the dining room door which was already opened

stephen was now sitting on the sofa near the dining room table this time he had his jeans on,he was looks looking through is mobile phone he had in his hand

morning stephen,did you sleep alright

yeah morning alex,I not long got up,he said taking his eyes

off the phone watching his brother walk in to the room to the dining room table which still had stephen's coffee cup on it with Jaycees empty glass including jaycee's mobile phone with car keys

my sleep was okay,I could of gotten a bit more still,he said to alex

alex took a chair at the table

so where's jaycee,he asked his brother,who's eyes were back looking at his mobile scrolling through the recieved messages

oh he just went upstairs to get a quick wash and stuff

i'm going up after him,stephen continued to say

okay answered alex,as the both of them could hear lucy moving items in the kitchen

stephen put his mobile onto the sofa got up walked to the dinning room table picked up his cup with the empty glass

let me take these into the kitchen,he said ,

while alex sat there with one hand in his hair playing feeling fumbling about with his little dreadlocks which covered the whole of his head.

Upstairs jaycee had just entered the bathroom closing the door behind him luis had just gone back into his bedroom carlos was still laying on the bed but he weren,t sleeping,he was laying on his side one hand underneath the back of his head helping him to hold up supporting his head up from off the pillow watching miguel walk in shutting the door

your looking nice and fresh bruv,he said laying there looking a bit tired faced

luis was drying himself down with the towel he had brought with him slowly walking towards the closed curtains pulling them open one curtain at a time holding onto his towel it's time to get up bruv,he said to carlos

his eyes looking through the white netted curtains which covered the window out at the street down below where he could see a few parked up cars on either side of the road with carlos and jaycee,s car knowing to himself there were a lot more cars parked up in this street last night when they all strolled through into lucys home in the early hours of the morning

anyone using the bathroom ? carlos asked him as he stood there at the window looking out while drying himself with his towel

yeah jaycee has just gone in there and there's probably going to be a queue for the bathroom bruv

because there's only one bathroom in this house

I was the first in there,

okay carlos answered,moving his hand from the back of their head laying his head back down onto the pillow

luis flung the towel over his shoulder picking up his rucksack just a few feet from him now in search for some body spray with deodrants

            Mark was now out of his bedroom walking the landing opening up the towel cupboard taking out a towel then closed it back the he stood outside of the bathroom door asking who was in there ?

it's jaycee,the voice inside said

okay jaycee knock my rooms door when you have finished so I can use the bathroom it's the only bedroom door on the right of the landing

okay,came jaycees answered

mark walked back to his room waiting for Jaycee to knock

his waiting wasn't for long it was only a few minutes before the door knocked

mark hearing jaycee's voice outside,saying the bathroom was now ready,

jaycee put his used towel in the plastic clothes basket before getting into his trousers then brushed his teeth taking a quick shower,he was now walking down the stairs into the dining room where he found alex and stephen there

you alright guys,he said as soon as he walked in i'm feeling more awake now,i'm going to my car to get something,he continued saying walking to the dining room table picking up his car keys then looked towards stephen on the sofa saying,we've got to be leaving after breakfast i've got to be back in london mate

yeah I hear you,stephen responded

okay jaycee said,then left the room walking to the front door to his car returning back in minutes closing the front door behind him entering into the dining room once again smelling strongly of aftershave which he left in his car

the then took a chair at the table next to alex

let me see if lucy need some help with the breakfast,stephen said getting up from the sofa walking to the kitchen door opening it walking in then closing the door

as soon as the kitchen door shut the front door started knocking

let me go ands see who it is, alex said,getting up leaving the table going through the hallway to the front door opening it

what a nice surprise,he said seeing his four neices standing out by the front door all looking at him

hi uncle alex ,zoe the oldest neices said then sister letita then clouie and courtney before they all walked in through the the

front door

where's auntie lucy? zoe asked her uncle

she's in the kitchen

they all took off their coats in the hallway alex closed the front door

hanging their coats on the coat hanger attached to the hallway wall before all four walked into the dining room

oh this is uncle stephen's friend his name is jaycee

alex said walking in behind them introducing them each by name

saying this is niece zoe letita clouie and courtney

letita said happily excitingly

ho my uncle stephen is here also

yes he's in the kitchen with auntie lucy

all four of them walked to the kitchen door opening it with a large smile on their faces.

CHAPTER 62   ON THE JOURNEY

His foot had been pressed down on the accelarator pedal throughout most of the journey on the M4 almost 90 % of the time in the front lane only moving into the middle lane if the traffic was moving to slow due to other cars up ahead in the fast lane not considering the car behind needing to overtake so in realsing the delay seeing the speed dile falling back down moving forward he would slip into the second lane even the first lane illegally overtaking until he passed the tourist driver or he would call them sunday drivers delaying everyone in the fast lane

he was glad now to be entering the north circular having been driving constantly for a long while his passenger driver had fallen asleep a good hour ago the sweet R amd B music playing through the music system must of given him an helping hand,he would be surprised when he woke up where he now was,as the driver drove on with no delay finding shorter routes with short cuts to the destination ahead

The car driver drove on feeling glad in himself,the roads were all dry,it was another 35 minutes before the driver took his foot completely of the accelarator pedal pulling up his handbrake putting the gear into neutral before looking at his passenge still asleep in his seat while the music played on now at a moderate not to high level

hay birdy wake up man,i'm parked up outside your home front door,jaycee said undoing his seat belt could allowing a little free space to strech himself a little,moving himself up and down before he continued the journey which would be next to his home for the night.

Earlier at lucy home after everyone was served a plate of breakfast Stephen alex mark jaycee luis and carlos all took their seats some at the table others on the sofa,the four neices helped to bring the breakfast in to them helping lucy then lucy sat on the sofa with her husbands vernon opposite the dining table with their breakfast on their trays on their laps the four nieces sat on the sofa to the far wall near the kitchen,the dining room was filled with talk and laughter all the uncles glad to see their nieces which they hadn't seen since their other neice yasmins wedding in Swansea City two and a half years ago.

Yasmin was jeans daughter,now that the neices had turned up stephen told jaycee not to leave after their late breakfast for london but to chill out for a hour or more so he could get to spend a little time with his nieces,he already knew luis and carlos were not going back today after mark had told stephen he wasn't going back to bristol until tomorrow with luis and carlos

mushroom picking he said,in a low voice at the table,then smiled at his brother

alex had made up his mind to stay to stay at lucy's until tomorrow and make his way back to bristol in carlos car .

As the time moved onwards stephen and jaycee left

jaycee wheel spinning out of lucy's street as stephen thought to himself here we go again

putting on his seat belt strapping himself up like he was about to race in the Grand Prix racing car finals.

Now here he was being woken up by jaycee not even realsiing he had fallen asleep were outside your front door birdy,jaycee said again

birdy now awake surprised to see he was home already

door step delivery,birdy said looking across at Jaycee,well atleast I got back in one piece at a record breaking time,he continued to say,then gave a little laugh

yeah nice one jaycee,birdy said undoing his seatbelt

call me yeah and get home saftely,he said opening the passenger door jumping out then clenched his one fist leaned a little forward into the car then spudded jaycee by knocking his fist

okay birdy bless jaycee said,

birdy stepped away from the car walk back around his car onto the pavement

birdy could hear the reevs reviving up as jaycee slammed his car into gear lift up the clutch pedal slamming his foot down onto the gas pedal

beep beep with a big loud wheel spin then he was off once again.

CHAPTER.63   OUT
IN THE ELEMENTS

Everything was nice peaceful and very quiet inside of lucy's home the only thing could be slightly heard was the sound of raindrops pitter pattering on the window of her home this early tuesday morning the early winter rains were on their way and now here,the warm temperatures of the autumn had come to it's end,the house themometer dropping every other day slowly closing into the minus degrees but not yet arriving there as yet, outside on the roads and streets it was very cold but not freezing the air was bitter cold,he season for their scarfs and gloves to keep yourself warm and comfortable out there.

If you listened carefully then another noise you would detect coming from upstairs in one of the bedroom the noise was coming from lucy,s room the noise of snoring lucy wasn't the one doing the snoring the noise of snoring travelled through the bedroom door onto the upstairs landing starting to fade away halfway down the stairs so whoever was sleeping downstairs escaped the noise of snoring.

Downstairs in the front room alex was asleep on the sofa wrapped up under his sheet with a electric two bar heater on keeping the room nice and warm while it's curtains were closed,in the room next door which was the dining room both sofa were back to their usually order the dining room was empty

Back upstairs the room opposite to lucy's bedroom

which mark was in also luis and carlos room where both empty for right now mark was leading the way through the wet muddy steep hills in an area in port talbot called baglan, taking one carful step up at a time holding onto thin tall trees while pushing wet bushes with stingy nettles aside from him luis and carlos follwed in his tracks as the early morning rains continued to fall carlos had parked his car on one of the streets further down the mountain.

It will be on the right over there mark said,sitting in the passenger seat pointing at the last street the street which was the most furthest up the mountainous green hills giving them all lot less of a climb even though it was still a steady climb up to the mushroom fields,luis and carlos had their long thick winter jackets on but were not wearing suitable foot ware for this type of wet rainy morning weather,both wearing sports trainers which weren't the best dress code for climb-ing the hills in this weather,the best dresscode would be a nice thick water proof jacket or rain coat some water proof trou-sers and wellington boots would be the perfect foot wear.

The rains were still falling but not so heavy when they parked the car up in the last street on the mountain side,all getting out of the car carlos locking it up carlo wore a thick woollen hat on his head luis covering his head with the hood of his jacket so to did mark the day light had only just started to break through,now separatly the night darkness causing it to slowly vanish bringing in this new wet morning as the three of them made their way out of the street all had a few plas-tic carrier bags tucked away inside of their jackets and trou-sers pockets hoping by the time they were leaving the baglan mountains atleast one or two bags would be filled up with magic mushrooms.

Luis and carlos had never experienced climbing a mountain before they were use to the concrete jungle stoney building city life always trying to keep themselves looking clean groomed smooth and tidy,dirt free not being use to dirt mud with gunge,they followed mark in through a dirt pathway in the now light falling rain which took them to the mountain side this way boys,mark hollared,signaling his hand,turning around to make sure they both were still up with his walking pace

okay,luis said

tagging along next to carlos following mark in the rain in the country of wales in a town he had only been in a few days called port talbot town

he walked onwards realsing every single step forward he made the hill got steeper and steeper,he looked down at his sport trainers they were looking soaking wet with the rain,he continued on ,their progress was slow but steady

we are going to have to cut through those woods over there, mark shouted pointing his hand towards the direction just a little further up on the left side of the dirt track they all had been walking along for about 10 minutes

okay,luis said

but you know what mark,luis said as mark stood his ground about 10 feet from them waiting for the both of them to catch up to him

thinking to himself they both were moving way to slow

what,s that mark asked,while he stood there

luis walking closer to him carlos Just a few seconds behinds

my bloody legs are aching me,luis said sounding a little out of breath and mine are carlos repeated sounding a little tired also

well we will all be there soon,we are half way there now mark told them but remember this mark said still standing there allowing them both to get a few moment of rest before they all started off again

once you get to the top then there is no more climbing also going back down the mountain is a peace of cake,okay lets go then,he said moving forward again further up the ever growing steeper dirt pathway then he crossed over to his left entering the woods which were filled with hundreds of thin tall trees everywhere,the rains continued to fall the three of them could feel their trousers were slowly getting soaked they could also feel the wet coldness of the rain soaking through their trousers and jeans onto the skin of their legs but they continued on starting pushing their way through the woods holding onto certain trees for their suppoort using them to pull themsleves further up and forward every once in a while mark luis and carlos would find their feets slipping then sliding from underneath them because the grass with earth beneath their feets were now made very slippery due to the morning rains,now their footwear was hardly recognisable covered all over with wet grass smalll twigs leaves and dirt while they continued on up to the magic mushroom fields pushing branches from trees filled with wet leaves out of their faces as mark stepped on taking the lead.

alright we've made it,luis could hear mark say standing now on another dirt pathway after just climbing out from the woods filled with mud and wet trees

luis stepped onto the pathway then carlos followed seconds later

so we are here then?luis questuioned mark,while the three of them stood on the dirt pathway

no not yet weve just made it through the woods,mark told them

how far now bruv ? luis asked,feeling anxious also wet legged with his socks all soaking wet in his sports trainers because of the wetness of the grass with mud not wearing the proper protective foot wear

Carlos felt so worn out he didn't even have a single word to say,he was just hoping this miserable nightmare would be over very soon now thinking that if he was in london he wouldn,t be halfway up a mountain soaking wet and freezing cold searching for magic mushrooms for he would be tucked away nice warm comfortably inside of his double bed whether on his own or companied with one of his sexy lady friends,but out of respect to help his friend luis who kept banging on about we must pick some magic mushrooms so we can take them back to london with us he went a,long with it but only if he knew before hand the journey on foot you had to go through to get to even just one of it's fields he definitely would of said,no way

well it was too late and could only now put it all down to a new experience to himself.

Mark stood on the new dirt track his jacket hood covering his head his trousers wet his foot wear unrecognisable but it didn,t seem to bother him in the slightest,while the rain started to ease its falling he looked at luis and carlos,smiled at them then said,we've done good guys,most of the climbing is nearly done now,all we have got to do now is,he said,turning around now pointing to a small steep hill which stood right across the dirt track right infront of them

we climb right up there then were home,the field is on top of this last hill we will be up it in 5 minutes man,okay he finished.

◆ ◆ ◆

CHAPTER
64   DRUGS

Drugs fill up our material world

hard drugs with soft drugs too

drugs which will speed up your heart beats

even drugs which will make you hallucinate

bringing paronoia into your mental view

    Class A drugs sold on the streets

    in the big busy cities also in the villages with towns

    they are being used by asll types of people

    not just the under-priviledge people

    living underground

It's a billionaire business enterprise

being secretively brought into the country

from all parts of this world

South America the Carribean Europe Africa

to some people it's like liquid gold

    It may seem inexpensive

    looking very cheap to many

    for they only ever see classs A drugs

    in tiny little bits

while it is being smuggled over into countries

inside plans trains lorries boats even sailing ships

Those who are not affected by any street drugs

should count themselves as very fortunate also lucky

for I have witnessed with my own very eyes

how it has stripped bare

the self respect with dignity of many

Hard drugs it desrtroys,it ruins lives

it certainly does transform

turning you into something strange

of which you were not

suppose to be born into then formed.

It will turn the strong weak

it will turn the fit unhealthy

you will not be walking around

with a fresh innocent face

it will as time moves forward

look unhealthy even guilty

Its not wise neither is it sensible

to get yourself involved with any kind of drugs

for soon you will see the only people

you will be surrounded around

will be dodgy characters crooks

thieves with unloyal thugs

It's great business for the heartless criminal minded

they can make hundreds of thousand's

also millions of pounds at a time

while those simple minded of the poor people

buy up the drugs in small amounts

now going through the process

of slowly losing their minds

    Drugs don't physically

    neither mentally build you up

    little by little slowly but surely

    in time they will bring you down

    all those drug free

    belonging to the daily common people

    when they see you coming in the futuristic time

    they will see you are far away

    from looking perfect and sound

So please leaving the drugs alone

didn't you know most time soft drugs

leads onto more harder drugs

we wish to see you standing steady stable also strong

knowing under your feet

have been pulled away that comfortable rug.

◆ ◆ ◆

CHAPTER 65

IN THE HILLS

Mark had just reached the top of the final hill,which took him to the very top of baglans mountain,he was glad to know all the climbing was now all over,he stood up straight at the beginning of the field he was now standing in then took in a deep breath of the country air,while old memories of his early teenage years started flowing through the memory lane of his mind in the mid 1990's when his young youthfull legs with feets use to climb these very hills every september october and novemnber with his friends all eager in the search for the magic mushrooms,he had forgotten until now the struggle it use to take them all to get to the top but once the challenge was complete there was always then only good things to expect,he was hoping now this morning the results would turn out to be exactly the same while he now watched carlos now tiredlessly climbing up the last few steps to the top of the mountain to the beginning of the mushroom field with him the only thing which separated the both of them from the mountain side with the fields was a wire fencing which was only around four feet high,most all other surrounding fields on the mountain top were separated by this wire fencing the only reason mark thought the wire fencing was put up was to control the farm animals so they just couldn't just wander off into any field.

There were farm yards hidden up there in the mountains some would be clearly spotted depending how far across the top of the mountain you walked it was another world up there compared to being back down there in port talbot town with the other surrounding neighbouring towns with villages,up in the mountains was were the real country life and living was you would find fields filled with cows some with a bull here and there,fields with sheeps some with horses all grazing away in the fields while on other occassions if your eyes were quick enough to notice you would notice that you have been noticed by a sly peeping fox or two or a dear.

Luis eventually arrive at the top,the three of them now still standing on the outside of the fence their backs now leaning and bouncing against the wired fence,they looked down at the scenery of the town below from where he stood they could see nearly all of the town looking at the A48 with the traffic flowing pass the edge of the town on the left and right of the A48 even at his time this morning it was very busy.

Mark could see fairfield estate the area lucy's home was,he could also see the whole of sandfields estate the biggest estate in the town then the seafront with the sea stretching right out into the horizon circulating itself towards the right all the way over to the nearest city to port talbot which was swansea city,from where they all were standing mark coulds see swansea bay

luis took his mobile phone out so to did carlos while they stood there they started taking a few pictures so they could store it in their gallery for rememberance.

come on then guys,mark said,watching them both taking picture's then said we are not up here as tourists with a little laughter before he started to climb over the fence into the field then stood on the otherside inside of the field pulling out his plastic bag from one of his front jacket pockets,the field he was now standing in was a large field having no animals inside of it's field inbetween the wet green grass you could see that a flock of sheeps could not of very long ago been grazing in this field for there were sheep droppings everywhere also you could see four very tall steel electric pillions which each stood up atleast 75 feet in the air each about 75 feet away from each other all sharing electric cables standing in this field it was these pillions which directed mark to the mushroom field from the time Carlos had parked up his car down below on the mountain street.

Luis and carlos both climbed the fence into the field

yeah guys get your bags ready this is one of the magic musghroom fields we are standing in right now

let me see if I can find one to show you what they look like so you will know what you got to be picking

you don't want to be filling your bags with the wrong mushrooms

yeah luis and carlos answered

following mark watching him walk now on level ground on top of the mountain very slowly low down in a crouching position looking down at the ground where there was low growing grass also in places where the grass was grown he was moving slowly while looking all around where he crouched and walked

it took him less than a minute before luis and carlos heard mark say here we are guys look here as they were both right near watching him stopping by a cluster of strange looking mushrooms right next to a big toadstole mushroom

I got some here,he said pointing to them

allowing luis and carlos to have a goods look at them before he pulled them up one at a time counting them while putting them into his plastic bag these are them this is what they look like !

they were not very large in size their stems were about two to three inches in height with a dark black umberalla shape top at the end of it's stem

okay so these are the magic mushrooms then ? luis replied

they sure are mark answered then spoke on saying they look this colour because of the rain falling but later on if we are still up here and the sun comes up the tops may turn a white colour but these are them,okay

what we will do is start in this field stay in it for about an hour if it's a good field we should atleast pick two to three hundred mushrooms each,you only need to take atleast 40 mushroom for a decent proper trip,we will see how it goes from here okay.

CHAPTER
66   AT BIG SIS

The rain had stopped falling nearly one and a half hours ago the morning times slowly now being transformed into the early afternoon hours by the looks of how this day had started you would next expected to be seeing the sun showing its bright glowing face today but you would be wrong for the sun was now out clearly to be seen in the heavens even though its strong warm rays could not be felt,it still brought a little pleasantness to this days early afternoon hours.

The time on the dining rooms clock on lucy's dining room wall was on the move lucy had just come in from the concrete paving stone back garden after taking advantage of the little sunshine hanging washed clothe out on the clothing line,she had a young visitor in her living room who had called at her home a short time ago,it was her nephew luke roy her brothers son he was now sitting in the living room on the sofa opposite the dining room table sitting next to his uncle alex who sat beside him on the sofa.

Luke had got the news from his sister's who tried phoning him and ashley who was stephen's son when they were at aunt lucy's yesterday,but both their phones were off,so after leaving lucy's they went to lukes home finding him there with his parnet and young child,telling him his uncle alex and uncle mark were at aunt lucys home and uncle stephen had come down back had gone back to london today,luke told them he would pass to see his uncles tomorrow morning after zoe told him his uncles would be staying overnight,then next day he called around aunt lucys home and here he was now sitting on the living rooms sofa talking with his uncle alex while waiting for uncle mark to walk through the front door,lucy's husband vernon was back in on his favourite sofa watching the TV.

While coming down from the baglan mountains at a fast pace while trying hard to prevent themselves from falling was mark luis and carlos mouths filled with shouts of joy mixed with laughters as they bumped into trees having at times to hold onto some trees so they didn't tumble over, they had gotten down the first hill safetly to the dirt track then before they all knew it they had gotten quickly down through the woods onto the second dirt path where they all walked that dirt route together with a plastic bag each filled with magic mushrooms,they had counted around 800 magic mushrooms between them while picking them and counting them as they droped them into their plastic bags they were all happy with what they were now taking away with them even though they would of stay up there in the mushrooms fields a lot longer if they weren't hungry and thirsty for they hadn't eaten anything since they had woken up this morning,before they knew it they were back inside of carlos car driving back to lucys home mission accomplished.

CHAPTER 67 UNEXPECTED VISITOR

A few hours later that day back at lucys home things were very busy and active for it weren't to long after mark luis with carlos arrived back mark surprised to see his nephew luke at lucys home,introducing luke to luis and carlos.

A short time later lucy got another unexpected visitor knocking on her front door of her home,opening it finding lynette deeble coming to pay her a friendly family visit she was related to the Bird family through marriage to standford bird nephew stanford birds older sister sue bird's son,he was lynettes husband at the time,lucy gladly invited lynette in the both of them going into the front room vernon then leaving his favourite sofa going into the dining room so lucy and lynette could have a good old chat.

Mark luis and carlos had driven first to the drive through Mc Donald's on the waty back to lucys home making a decision among themselves to get some fast foods to fill their stomachs buying some burgers with french fries with a milkshake each,eating it once they got back to lucys,they all left their plastic bags of magic mushrooms in the back of the car by the orders of mark telling them his sister wouldn't be pleased to have anything to do with or connected to drugs in her home even if they looked like silly little mushrooms

you can count them properly when you get back to london or

when you are back at alex's flat,he told them

that's no problem,luis said,while he sat there in the back seat of the car

yeah okay carlos finished saying,sitting there in his car eyes looking out ahead of him at the few cars waiting in the queue to get their Mc'Donald's too.

All were now in the dining room talking until lynette arrived vernon then joining up in the dinning room while lucy and lynette talked away in the front room.

Stephen can remember lynette from he was a youg grow-ing child the early young years when he was growing up in port talbot,he knew lynette and his mother were very close spending many hours talking away the passing moving hours of the days while their children were in the infants with jun-ior schools in the early 1970's she was well respected by all the Bird family children for they all knew the respect lynette had shown towards their mother and this they all intended to show her for it was what she deserved.

Alex and mark came into the front room saying their hello's to lynette so did their nephew luke,lynette stayed for a few hours in the front room drinking tea while having a good laugh causing lucy to laugh until her stomach ached that late afternoon and early evening had gone well lynette was now about to go home,she lived in the margam area which was about one and a half miles away

I will see if one of the visitors who drive can give you a lift home if thats ok,lynette,lucy said as lynette walked out into the hallway to get her coat of the coat hanger

no it will be fine the bus station is not to far away as you al-ready know

no lucy insisted,you wait here let me make some use out of some of these young guys for once,she said then walked off into her dining room leaving lynette in the hallway putting her coat on

in seconds mark and carlos were walking out into the hallway

hi lynette,

carlos who was walking right behind him

mark said to her,carlos is going to drop you home I will be coming with him

oh thank you my dear

thats no problem my name is carlos,he said stretching his hand out towards her

lynette smiled then said thank you carlos,shaking his hand, saying nice to meet you as they were shaking hands lucy came out into the hallway with luis,

lynette she said,this here is luis he is carlos friend I would like to introduce you to,the both are down here on a visit from london they are my brothers friends

nice to meet you luis,she said,then they both shook hands

mark opened the front door turning around seeing luis shaking lynettes hand he then walked out with carlos

I will walk lynette to your car he told carlos,can you take thoses plastic bags filled with mushroom out and give them to luis to put upstairs for now

okay carlos said turned walking back to the front door seeing lynette and luis now walking out the front door with lucy standing by the front door

mark stood near the car

this way lynette he said,directing her to the passenger side of carlos car,which was on the road side the car was just parked right outside by lucys home,carlos told luis to come to the car which he did then opened it wait here bruv,he said

then opened his back door went into the back seat taking up the plastic bags of magic mushrooms giving them to luis

mark walked to the car with lyneytte,

lucy was still standing by the front door watching as luis walked toward her carrying three small plastic bags in one hand,she made a little space seeing he wanted to come back into her home,not thinking anything strange about the bags in his hand.

allow the lady to sit here please,you can sit in the back carlos said

no problem mark said,holding the passenger door open watching lynette climb into the car making herself comfortable then he closed the door for her then opened the back door of the car climbed in noticing lucy still standing by the front door of her home watching them all now inside of the car ready to drive away then,

luis suddendly appeared beside her before the car started to move.

◆ ◆ ◆

0.68   CURIOSITY

n Luis took the three bags of magic mushrooms upstairs putting them in the bedroom he and Carlos used on floor near the window then left the room closing the door walking back through the landing down the stairs through the short hallway standing back at the front door where lucy stood watching carlos start up his car engine lucy started to wave her bye byes to lynette

luis stoods there smiling watching carlos driving forward out of the street,he gave one single wave while lucy waved on until the car turned right out of the street

okay lucy i'm going back into the dining room,luis said then walked back into her home

lucy closed her front door then walked into her front room picking up the plastic tray which had two empty cups on it from off the little small table which was near the sofa in the room walking then out into the hallway then back into the dining room with a smile on her face passing luke alex and luis and her husband walking on into the kitchen with the tray in her hand leaving the kitchen door open as it already was.

Vernon who was sitting at the table in the dining room got up from his chair while alex and luke were sitting on the sofa near the table talking he walked back into the front room taking his position back in his sofa to watch the tv,luis was sitting on the sofa further back in the dining room near to the kitchen when lucy went into the kitchen while he sat there watching vernon get up walking out of the room,he then looked at alex and luke talking together

he got up from the sofa,the spirit of curiosity taking hold of him

walking pass alex and luke to the dining rooms entrance door,

he said i'm going upstairs for a few minutes alex

alex looked at him nodded his head while continuing to talk with his nephew

luis walked on through the dining rooms door turning left then walked up the stairs onto the top landing then towards his bedroom opening the door walking in closing the door behind him,walking straight over to the plastic bags picking his one up which was a blue colour plastic bag he was putting his magic mushrtooms into on the baglan mountain

he sat on the bed with the bag in his lap opened the plastic bag looked inside at a mass of magic mushrooms all stuck twisted up together inside for a few moments,sitting there staring into the bag looking at these strange looking mushrooms,they all looked soggy and moist they looked like they needed dry-ing out

mark had told him although they could still be eaten like that,

he put his hand into the bag pulling apart a single mushroom from the mass holding it in his fingers bringing it close to his face so he could get a better look at it,placing the plastic bag on the side of the bed

mm,he said then brought the mushroom under his nose giving it a sniff,

it had a peculair smell,he thought,he then put it onto his lap then pulled out a second one wiping the traces of little bits of green grass from off it putting this one also on his lap,then took out a third one cleaned of the grass going back into the plastic bag,he kept on doing this until he got to his 40th magic mushroom scrambling them all together now holding them all in one of his hand,getting up putting the plastic bag back on the floor next to the other plastic bags,before he left the room closing the door holding a hand full of magic mushrooms.

Walking straight to the bathroom opening the door walked in then locked the door behind him walking over to the wash basin turning on the cold water tap cusped his both hands together placing his hands under the slowly flowing water allowing the water to wash the mushrooms while using his two thumbs to move the magic mushrooms around in the palms of his hand,he did this for a few minutes until they looked clean from any dirt or tiny bits of grass then pulled his hands away from the tap keeping it running while squash-ing all the magic mushrooms together into one hand,opening his hand he looked at what now looked like a round ball of squashed mushrooms,the next thing the whole ball of magic mushrooms were inside of luis mouth,he bit it in half in his mouth until his teeth quickly realisied it seemed a little bit to much,spitting half the size of the ball back out into the palm of his hand allowing then his tongue to bring the other half to the back of his throat then he swallowed it with no hesitation quickly putting the second half back into his mouth doing the same thing with his tongue bringing it right to the back of his throat then swallowed it

yuk,he could hear his own mouth say at the taste of it in his mouth his hand went under the turned on tap as his other hand picked up the soap bar,he washed both hands putting the soap back to where it belonged then turned the tap off

thats that then he said,show me what you got then,he said laughing to himself in secret concerning the magic mushrooms walking to the bathroom door unlocking it leaving it slightly opened then walked back to the bedroom walked inside quickly to dry his hands with his towel he had early place on the radiator then left the room to go back down stairs into the dining room.

CHAPTER
69   TRIPS

About twenty five minutes later carlos parked his car back outside of lucy's home front door,that was a nice quick drive,he said pressing his foot onto the foot brake placing the gears into nutruel pulling up his handbrake undone his seat belt then looked towards his left at mark who said

yeah just a quick outing atleast lynettes got home safetly,thats the main thing mark replied while he undone his seat belt

your going to have to get them back from luis and bring them back to the car

yeah I will do that right now carlos answered

okay lets just keep them altogether in your car boot until we get back to bristol because you got my brother coming back up with us,mark continued to say sitting there in the passenger front seat looking straight at carlos

ok no probplem bruv,carlos said nodding his head in argreement

so what's happened to your mate carl?he's disappeared hasn't he phoned you or not is he coming back up to bristol with you when I drop you and alex back there

I dont know what he's up to carlos,he hasn't phoned me,I may phone him soon and find out because we won't be hanging around for to long and I know you guys want to get back to london,anyhow you best talk to luis and get those plastic bags into the boot,mark said finally before opening the passenger door climbing out

carlos opened his car door as mark was shutting his walking then around the front of the car onto the pavement to lucy's front door knocking it a few times while carlos closed his car door locking it then stood up right next to mark,a few seconds later the front door opened

alright mark the voice of vernon said

alright carlos he said,looking at the both of them then stepped to the side of the wall on his left giving them both enough space to walk in pass him both saying alright vernon before walking into the dining room,vernon shut the front door then walked back into the front room where his wife lucy now was.

as soon as mark entered the room he said,alright alex alright luke to the both of them sitting on the sofa then took a chair at the table looking then further into the room towards luis who was sitting on the other sofa looking calm and very relaxed

you alright luis mark said loudly

yeah I'm cool luis answered as carlos walked further into the room walking right up to the sofa luis was sitting on then sat right beside him

he then said in a normal but low tone of voice

hay luis you are going to have to get those bags of mushroom-s,here are my car keys he said,handing his keys over to him

mark watched them while carlos told luis to put the bags in the boot of his car then give him back the keys

okay luis said no problem bro,taking the keys then got up off the sofa looking at carlos with a big wide strange unusaul smile on his face looking wide eyed

carlos looked at him then thought as he looked into luis eyes that luis pupils were looking strangely large,he thought noth-ing else of the matter

luis walked away from his presence out of the dining room walking up the stairs along the landing into his bedroom picking up all the bags of magic mushrooms then went back downstairs opened up the front door holding the three bags of mushrooms in his hand with carlos car keys,he pressed the boot button on the electronic key device in his hand,the boot opened he put the three bags inside closed the boot then walked back into lucys home closing the front door walk-ing straight back into the dining room thinking these magic mushrooms he had taken are rubbish,I have eaten forty of them and I dont feel a thing,they should be working their powers on me by now,he thought walking pass alex and luke and mark to his seat on the sofa

here you are bruv,he said,chucking the car keys to carlos

nice one carlos said,catching them

luis sat there

so are we ready for the road ? carlos said

when you and them lot are ready,alex and mark,he mean't but carlos understood,

mark and hay alex's you guy are going to have to get yourself ready because we will be leaving this town soon,luis said sit-ting there

yeah we will be out of here in the next hour he then heared mark say

as luis stomach started bubbling and feeling strange

mm,he thought then shrugged of any thoughts chuckling a lit-tle to himself because of the funny feeling looking to his left at carlos sitting next to him,

his friend carlos face was now covered all over in thick white cobwebs,luis frooze in his sitting position having now to take harder look rubbing his eyes quickly clearing it then looked at carlos again,

whats happening,he said to himself,carlos his face was still covered all over with thick white cobwebs

carlos,he said

whats the matter carlos said in a deep hollow sounding tone of voice in slow motion looking now like a dead corpse sitting there next to him,he then looked over at mark at the dining room table,he couldn't believe what he was now staring at, mark looked like a little ten year old child sitting at the table looked at luis even alex also and luke looked as young as mark they had all turned into little children

whats up luis,mark spoke in a little child like voice,then laughed at him with a boyish laughter

vernon walked into the dining room his face was also covered all of with cobwebs looking like a corpse,luis was now filled with fright and panic thinking is this a dream it must be a dream this is a nightmare,its time to wake up,the clock in the living room by the dining table on the wall started to tick extremely loud every tick sounded like a beat on a wooden drum which could not be ignored,luis heart was now beating frantically in his chest terror now took hold of him he got up from the sofa without saying a single word to anyone in the room as vernon said in a deep hollow slow motioned voice,I am going to make myself a nice hot drink,

luis mind started thinking,*drink think brink link* ryhmns,he thought

while walking towards the dining rooms door passing mark who sat at the table still looking like a junior school kid looking at him laughing constantly while luke and alex were laughing also they to still looked like little boys,he thought *boys toys noise spoils soil*,he now realised he couldn't think straight he couldnt get his thoughts straight his head was filled with rythmns *times mind bind blind slide find*

I got to get out of here,he said,*gear steer dear rear tear fear near* while he walked into the hallway to the front door opening it then walked out of the front door leaving it wide open.

CHAPTER
70   TRIPPING

Luis found himself fleeing down the street's of port talbot in the evening still believing he was in a dream this can't be real he was running,but why was he running,what was he even running from,he thought,*run gun none* this is *dumb*,he thought,is this real or is this a dream he thought,*sleep peep deep,*I want to *weep creep creepy,*he thought running on in fear all on his own get a *grip slip trip* thats it he know tried hard to think straight, *mushroom tomb soon doom womb* his mind keep rhymning words,he looked down at his feet on the grey concrete pavement curb *herb obsurb heard* was the words,he heard,is this what he desereved,he thought now struggling again with his thoughts

I must be tripping it's the mushrooms,its not a dream,he now thought as he stopped running,slowing his pace down to a walking pace,he must of been running for a few minutes through the streets of port talbot like a mad man,he looked at his dress wear,he had his trainers on jeans and top the evening air was cold it weren't raining the enviroment he was in felt weird strange canny,there were a few strangers walking in this street filled with houses on both sides of the street the street was lite up with street lights,he walked on as the few strangers walked close towards him ready to pass him,luis took a quick look at their faces as they passed by their faces were normal as they passed by talking with each other

okay today horray his thoughts did say while he walked on

up the street feeling very strange within himself a bit confused,he started believing in himself there was a very dangerous scarey clown hiding in the front seat of one of the
parked cars on this street who was soon going to open the
car door then suddenly scare frightening the life out of him,he
started looking in every single car parked on that street he
passed waiting for the clown to show his scarey face but the
clown didn't appear,he walked out of the street walking on
now thinking of lucy's home *zone alone dome moan* groan,these
thoughts started appearing in his mind,feeling mentally tired
he sat down on a small brick wall out the front of a house in
this new street he was in

uuuhh,you could hear him say getting back up straight away
because the wall felt liker jelly

the word jelly came into his mind *jelly belly kelly smelly nelly*
bloody crazy thoughts *crazy lazy daisy*

get back to friends,he thought,*friends ends tends mends send
bends* luis turned around started to walk trying to retrace his
steps back into the last street were he was now filled again
with the fear of the dread believing he would soon be attacked
by a scarey danger deadly clown hidden away in one of the
parked up cars waiting to jump out onto him

    He walked off the pavement starting now to walk up
the street filled with houses in the middle of the road until he
entered the next street hoping he weren't to far away from his
friends sister home,he stayed in the middle of the road while
he walked on forward with his mind still filled up with ryhmns flowing through his head trying his best to straighten out
his thoughts,*drugs thugs mugs bugs* after a little while he realised he had been walking down this empty street filled with
houses with some of their lights on lighten by streets light
with cars parked on both sides of the street for a little while
and still hadn't gotten to the end of this street while keeping himself fully alert while he still walked in the middle of

the road in the street carefully looking into the front street of every car he passed.

He kept walking and walking but seemed to be getting nowhere checking his pockets insearch of his mobile phone realising now he didn;t have it on him trouble,he thought, *double trouble rubble stubble bubble* he felt upset bothered really angry not knowing where he was while still walking down this which seem very long like a never ending street in the middle of it's road,which seem to have no end his eyes then notice a person on the left side of the pavement walking up the street towards his direction,so he started to walk back onto the pavement towards this person who he could now see was a female just by the way this person walked and was dressed as the person was about to pass him he took a quick look at the person once again fear took hold of luis when he realised the female didn,t even have a face no eyes no nose no mouth just a head filled with long flowing brown hair but no face,nightmare,he thought,then started running down this street hoping to get to the end of it which seem to be taking him forever.

CHAPTER
71   EARLIER

Back at lucy's home earlier mark had been looking at luis a bit strangely wondering what he had kept staring oddly at Carlos who was sitting next to him on the sofa,he started acting a litlte weird before leaving the dining room they all thought luis had gone upstairs to the bathroom or to the bedroom getting ready for the travel back to bristol then to london it was only when lucy came into the dining room from the front room asking who had left the front door wide open because the cold draft of the evening was coming in

what mark questioned,the front door is opened?

I thought vernon closed it when me and carlos me in

no it was opened,lucysaid while she stood in the hallway by the entrance of the dining room door

I just had to closed it,can you keep it closed please,she said before going back into the front room to ask Vernon did he close the front door properly

it was then mark looked towards carlos the both of them looking at each other like they could read each others thoughts

mark got up from his chair leaving the table carlos got up from the sofa mark then walked pass alex and luke who both didn't have a clue what was going on carlos just a little behind followed mark up the stairs,mark realising when he got to the top of the stairs the bathroom door was wide open,he looked in it was empty looking at carlos,

he said there's no one in there

walking then down the landing to the room carlos and luis shared

mark opened the door then just stood there,

carlos standing behind him,both looking into a empty room

he;s not there,carlos said

mark walked into the bedroom carlos followed closing the bedroom door behind them,mark turned on the bedroom light then looked down at luis green rucksack,then said let me check my room turning around walking passed carlos opening the bedroom door stepping out onto the landing walking the few steps to his bedroom opening the door switched on the light,the room was also empty,

it's empty,he said before turning back of the lights then closing the door,he had a quick look into his sisters bedroom right next door just to make sure there was no one in there,it was empty carlos stood by the room door that he and luis had shared watching mark checking the bedrooms then saying they are empty

so where the heck has he disappeared to mark uttered,walkiing towards carlo's then stood there looking at him

the only place he can be is in my car,but I got the car keys pulling them out from his pocket showing them to mark,then said unless he didn't lock the car when he put the bags of magic mushrooms back in there,

lets go check mark said,

the both of them walked off down the landing leaving the bedroom light on which had luis rucksack in there making their way down the stairs mark opened the front door then looked out at carlos car carlos came standing by the front door beside him they both could see his car which was only a few feet away empty,luis wasn't in there they both looked at each other looking surprised not even thinking what to say to each other for a moment

well atleast we know who left the front door opened now mark said then he turned from the front door about to walk back into the house then carlos,said we are going to have to go out looking for him,

let me get my phone and call him mark said,

yeah carlos replied watching mark walk into the house,he started following him,

make sure you shut the front door,mark said walking towards the dining rooms entrance to get his phone on the dining rooms table,carlos walked back to where he was sitting then said don't bother phoning him

why is that? mark questioned,now standing by the table holding his mobile phone in his hand

because his phone is here on the sofa,

what's up alex asked looking at his brother then at carlos

luis gone missing,he's not upstairs and he's not in the car

taking his chair now at the table

maybe he's gone to the shop arond the corner

he hasn't even been gone 10 minutes alex stated which was a possiblility mark and carlos thought

yeah I suppose your right mark answered,sitting there looking a little puzzled

mark also carlos both couldn't help looking at the time on their mobile phones every few minutes that now passed while waiting for the front door to knock

20 minutes had now passsed,that's it,Mark said to carlos alex and luke let's all go out looking for him,I don't know what's happened to him,maybe he's gotten lost coming from the shop,he doesn't know his way around anywhere in this town,he said standing now in the middle of the dining room looking at them all, carlos sat on the sofa,

he said you know what bruv,

whats that mark answered,turning his attentioin to carlos as he stood there in the dining room

do you think he's snealkly took some of those magic mushrooms and they have freaked him out,

mark looked at carlos,then thought for a moment then laughed to himself at his thoughts,then said,you know what it is a possibility because he was acting a little weird before he disappeared

yeah carlos said getting up picking up luis mobile phone putting it in his jeans pocket while holding his own mobile phone in his hand.

◆ ◆ ◆

no.72   ON A TRIP

The magic mushrooms had now taken full control of luis mind playing out performing it's illusions on his mind transforming while changing the enviroment around him which was already a strange forgein area, it had now become even more stranger,the world to him now seemed like legoland just like toy town,every street he now entered walking through in search of lucys home looked the same,he now walked like he was in a trance state his eyes were wide open while he walked pass people,walking by every now and then,taking a quick glance at them,they all had plastic toy like faces they didn't look human anymore some had square block faces some tri-angler face with big and small round faces with long and short necks,he tried speaking to one or two of these weird looking people but gave up after the second attempt when he realised every time he opened his mouth to speak no words came out.

He still couldn't get his thoughts properly together to even ask a question which seemd sensible even worse he didn't even know the name of the street lucy's home was on not even the name of the area,he knew he was lost not even having a clue were he was walking to,he didn't even know how long the effects of the magic mushrooms would last finding himself struggling to think and reason with his thoughts say-ing,not forever *clever never however,*

it had to eventually end,*friend mend bend,*his thoughts strug-gled he was trying to make sense of things walking along in his tranced state while looking around trying to find lucys street but still all the streets looked the same in toy town,the only thing which looked different were the people with their odd shaped heads with bodies,he came to a shop called SPAR

aahh,SPAR,he thought,then drink came to his mind *drink hint mint blink wink,*walking through the aisles in search of some-thing to drink,he spotted milk in the refrigarator shelves picked up a bottle queuing up with a lot off strange looking people in the queue patiently waiting his turn to be served,he gave the cashier money took his change then hurried out of the shop,opening the milk as soon as he left the shops entrance automatic doors he held his head back opened wide his mouth his throat felt very dry dyhdrated like all the moistness had been drain from it with also his tongue,he poured the milk into his mouth right to the back of his throat filling his mouth with the milk while he stood right outside by the entrance of the shop,he frooze in shock the milk had somehow turned into solid substance inside of his mouth,it now felt like a block of wood he quickly spat it out,his hand letting go of the milk bottle his eyes watching the bottle fall to the concrete ground in slow motion hitting the ground slowly smashing into pieces as most of the customers inside of the shop were now looking out at him,luis magic mushroom trip continued on.

CHAPTER 73
WONDERING

Carlos and mark were both baffled by the disappearance of luis it was now just over 6 hours he had been missing

alex and luke mark and carlos had given up looking for him out there after walking all around searching the streets shops with parks and alleyways of fairlield they walked on into the town centre up station road looking in all the wine bards and pubs on station road including Jimmys bar but there was no sign of him

he definitely must be tripping,mark jokingly said when alexs and carlos got back to lucys home with him their nephew luke had left them after they had given up the search he decided to go back to his own home.

alex laughed at what his younger brother just said

the three of them just took their seats in the living room after being let into the home by lucy.

you didn't find him then,she said noticing he wasn,t with them when she opened her front door looking at the three of them standing infront of them

we haven't got a clue where he is,alex replied as they walked back into the home one at a time now sitting in the dining room

carlos understanding the little joke shared between the brother's mark saying for luis to disappear at a time like this when they were all soon to be getting ready for the travel back to bristol then london he must be nuts,lucy didn't understand what he meant.

Lucy shut her front door behind them joining them in the dining room Vernon left the front room going into the dining room sitting on the table next to his wife,mark sat there at the table with them,alex was sitting back on the sofa near the dining room table carlos back on the sofa further down in the room

so what are you lot going to do now ? vernon asked mark

mark looked at alex then looked at carlos then said we don't Know we are just going to l have to wait a bit and see if he turns up,carlos said then continued saying I got no choice I just can't leave this town without him I came here with him I just can't drive out to bristol or to london without him

he's got his wallet with him hasn't he alex asked sitting there with his fingers in his black hair feeling and caressing his little locks on his head while he looked to his right at carlos

you know what I don't know

he probably does have his wallet if its not upstairs in the bed-room,let me go and check,carlos said,getting up then walking pass everyone out of the dining room to the stairs to the bedroom a few moments later he was back down the stairs in the dining room taking his seat back on the sofa telling them luis had left his wallet inside of his rucksack so where ever he was outside he was outhere with no money which made the situation more crazy and more worse they all stayed in the dining room talking minds fillled up with unanswered questions minds filled with wonders not even sure neither certain of what they should now do,they sat there puzzled.

CHAPTEER 74
DOWN TO EARTH

The effects of the magic mushrooms were now slowly starting to wear off from the mind of luis he could now slowly but surely feel himself slowly coming back down to earth slowly once again starting to feel himself feeling the normal feeling of just being able to be himself,his thoughts with thinking process connecting back up with the present realities now slowly being able to once again think properly and straight,he could even feel a smile of gladness appeaar on his face feeling a bit relieved while finding himself walking the main streets in port talbot station road not even realising how he had got there also not even knowing where he had been the last few passsing hours the only thing he knew was he was feeling nice,just like a person who was completely lost but had now found their way back on track ,a way out an escape route,he felt free.

He could feel freedom which was a sweet tender feeling to all of his senses his body was buzzing twingling twiting all over from the top of his head all through his neck arms body legs right down to his toes it felt alive like all of his nerves in his body were switched on and tenderly buzzing,luis laughed to himself as the thought of the scarey clown came to his mind

now believing also knowing it wasn't real but just his imagin-
ation playing tricks on him,even thought not very long ago those thoughts frightenend the life out of him,then he felt

threatened it felt very real

he walked on along station road now thinking to himself how was he going to find lucys home he didn't even know what the time was but he had that feeling knowing the time was pushing on and it must be very late in the evening nearing midnight

excuse me sorry mate,he said to a man standing outside Jimmys bar with a few of his fiends

what's the time pleased,luis asked

they guy looked at his watched told him the time

thanks mate,luis replied also feeling good in himself to know all those images of square headed triangled faced strange people had now turned back to normal faces

what a strange weird experience,he told himself as he started walking away from Jimmys bar down station road insearch of the right direction to lucys home so he could get back to his friends hoping they were all still there and hadn,t left the town without him

hay luis,he could hear a voice call from behind him

is he still tripping,he thought when he heard the voice calling his name he turned around to see who was calling him

luis what you doing up here he heard the voice say

luis could see carl standing outside the entrance door of Jimmys bar looking towards him smiling

where are the others carl shouted as he walked towards luis

i'm out on my own bruv,i've been tripping my head off on those magic mushrooms you and mark were telling me about

carl laughed,when he heard what luis had just said

so you did pick some then carl questioned standing there on the pavement a few feet down from Jimmys bar right next to luis yeah I picked and eat about forty of them i'm only now coming down from the mushroom trip they are craazy bruv luis said with a laugh i've never experienced anything like it, what a trip man,luis stated now knowing he had got pass the worst of his experience knowing now what to expect next time if he ever tried taking them again

so your going back to lucys home now are you ?carl asked

lucys home,luis stood there looking at carl then said

i'm lost man I don't know how to get back there

your lucky that I just came out of Jimmy's bar for a quick cigarette i'm in there with a friend Carl told him let me finish this cigarette,he said taking one out from the packet in his hand offering one to luis which luis took then gave luis the lighter after lighting his cigarette it was after a few minutes they both finished smoking luis then followed carl into Jimmys bar to the corner of the bar were his friend sat inbetween several seat with a pint of nearly finished beer on the table infront of him

carl introduced luis to his friend

hay luis this is curtis he said.

CHAPTER 75
WONDERING

Carlos sat there on the sofa in the far end of the room with his mind thinking on over time,lucy and vernon had gone upstairs to relax in their bedroom,mark and alex was in the dining room with carlos mark still sitting on one of the chairs at the dining room table,alex was still on the sofa near the table they had all packed up whatever belonging they had into carlos car a little while ago just to keep their minds of the situation they had now found themselves in all waiting while wondering what had happened to luis while having no way of contacting him also carlos knowing luis had no money on him to get back to london by coach or train if they all left port talbot.

They all sat in the dining room all ready to make the journey out of port talbot onto the A48 but couldn't go nowhere knowing luis was missing they were all stuck not knowing what to do when the front door started to knock

that might be him mark said,hoping it was him so their nightmares could be over

I hope so carlos replied,the both of them got up from where they sat at the same time mark walkling quickly out off the dining room towards the front door alex got up following behind carlos out of the dining room into the hallway,mark opened the front door seeing carl curtis and luis standing at the door

he was glad at what his eyes were now showing him as he

stood there ,where the heck have you been luis ? he said with a big welcoming smile showing on his face,we've all been worried about you man

carlos took in a deep breath feeling a sigh of relief come over him knowing now all the worrying with waiting was now all over

alex was just glad that it was luis standing out there

alright carl alright curtis,mark said come in boys,they all went back into the dining room mark making sure the front door was shut before joining them all in the room

luis laughed while explaining to them all what had happened to him and that mark was right he got freaked out by the magic mushrooms and he shouldn't of taken them on the sly he was glad he was now feeling nearly one hundred percent back to normal he just now had the giggles and couldn't help laughing a lot for no real reasons he was just feeling the feelings of happiness

yeah carlos this is carl's friend curtis,he said while he sat next to carlos on the sofa furthest in the room curtis sat on one of the chairs at the table next to mark and carl while alex sat back on the sofa near the table

everyone else in the room knew curtis alex and mark knew him for years he was just another name of many of the hustlers in the town who was always willing to take a chance or two in trying to make a quick buck but he had never been a problem to alex and mark

so what happened to you ?mark asked carl

what do you mean,carl asked

well from the time you left us on saturday night I haven't heard from you I know carl replied,i've been busy sorry man anyhow i'm staying in port talbot now its no more bristol for me for the time,i've been over at curtis house having a good drink while he's been busy doing his thing

luis heard what carl was just saying then was he interested in buying some in time from him in big amounts

i'm buying it on a regular i've got my contacts,he told luis they come all the way down from cardiff to trade to me theve got cracking stuff the best i've ever tried good prices to curtis said happily feeling a bit buzzed from all the pints of beer with in-take of drugs of all sorts he had been on through the evening and late night

my dealers name is Bulla he said I just bought a few ounces from him the other day

luis and carlos minds were now both opened wide listening to what curtis was saying

they both looked at each other then grinned as curtis spoke on,luis then stopped curtis in his tracks by saying hay curtis I know bulla your dealer

how do you guys know him when you lot are from london

its the reason we came down from london in the first place to drop off cocaine to Bulla which he sold to you luis said sitting there right next to carlos the both of them started laughing

curtis looked at the both of them,then said really your being serious

yeas luis said then discribed how bulla looked

so do you know the dread he asked luis

no I don't know his friend the dread but I know Bulla because Mark introduced Bulla to me,mark knowing bulla and the dread he was looking for a dealer and I am bulla's dealer he told curtis who was now really surprised

hay don't worry luis said,its a good thing on your side it means you dont need no middle man like bulla and the dread you can just buy it straight from me and carlos also at an even cheaper price its a no lose situation if you asre interested and willing to travel up to london to collect it

curtis said that sounds great I will ride up on my motorbike

luis and curtis exchanged phone numbers alex left the room going upstairs to let his sister know they were all ready to be leaving for bristol and that luis had now turned up and he was okay right now sitting downstairs in the dining rooom with carl and a friend of carls.

CHAPTER 76
MOVING ON

Back in bristol alex was now glad to be in his flat standing in his kitchen making a hot cup of chocloate at these late hours of the morning mark was in his room getting ready for his sleep underneath his quilt snuggled up nice and warm with the tv volume turned down on very low he felt tired knowing sleep time wasn't faraway,while he could hear alex making movements in the kitchen,luis and carlos had dropped the both of them off right outside,alex flat building complex before saying their byes then driving off with the car music playing away driving on to the M4 motorway connection to london city the both of them didn't have to be driving back to london tongiht they could of stayed at alex flat until tomorrow then travel back anytime tomorrow but carlos was saying he had been resting most of the day yesterday and with all that had happened with luis doing the vanishing act he just wanted to get back to london in no time so london was now their final destination.]

Carlos kept his eyes focused ahead with his foot down on the gas pedal taking in the music while luis sat there comfortable in the passenger seat now feeling exhausted and tired now after all that weird bizzare evening on the magic mushrooms he sat there slowly falling in and out of sleep somehow his mind went back to the days when he was in the prison system

Thinking of the times when marks cousin leroy was

on the seek for vengenace for him that afternoon when he had left the new job in the laundry factory being locked up back in his cell after collecting his dinner leroy had eaten his dinner then after leaving his empty silver stainless steel tray on the cell floor he leaned over on his iron bed resting himself knowing he would be unlocked again withing the next one and a half hour for work in the laundry factory for a few hours this afternoon he felt glad now that he had finally been given a job on the wing and even better still one of francis friend was working there who he intended to be applying some of his brutal pressure on whenever he got the oppurtunity.

Leroy laid there resting with a pleasant pleasing smile covering his face he felt excited glad he had something to focus his mind on someone to take his pent up anger out on someone who he believed deserved it and francis with all of his friends certainly fitted that catogory

he was also waiting for the early evening hours for assocation time to arrive so he could find out if his cousin mark had spoken to any of the prison officers to see if he could get transfered into marks cell or Mark transfered to his cell so they could share a cell together more than the both of them being in a single cell as they were

a little while later leroy was back downstairs in the laundry factory doing his new job separating dirty towels from dirty prison clothes in one of the big steel clothes containers putting the clothes in one large steel container and the towels in another while trying to keep his eyes on francis's friend who work close by him quickly realiasing the laundry factory would be no safe sensible place to be trying to attack anyone,there were to many eyes to many witnesses leroy now focused more on his job in the factory and more on the evening assocation which was to come which weren't forever away.

The afternoon had come and gone the evening meals were served out to all the landings that early evening one landing at a time all cells were banged up locked securely,all inmates now in their cells resting waiting for the 7.30pm association time.

Now the time had arrived the cell doors were being unlocked one landing at a time one cell door at a time the inmates all flooding out onto the landings voices of inmates and prison officers filled the prison wing the noises of feets on landings with feets up and down the ironstairs mingled in with the noises of keys rattling on long steel chains could be heard all around the wing inmates walking along with their big blue and yellow coloured plastic mugs in their hands with tea bags or coffee or maybe hot chocolate if they were fortunate enough to buy coffee or hot chocolate in the once a week canteen with a bag of sugar,once all cell doors were unlocked on all landings the wing would now be busy for the next one and a half hours with convicts on the ground floor playing on the pool table or on the wooden top football table game some sitting on wooden chairs along side these games just watching while smoking their cigarettes or roll up.

Mark was already at the stainless steel hot water urn waiting in the long queue to fill his big plastic mug which already had coffee powdermilk with sugar inside of it when luis joined the queue after mark had filled his mug with hot water from the urn,he left the urn then walked up standing beside luis in the queue talking with luis while luis waited for his turn to use the hot urn

alright boys got to get myself some hot water the voice of leroy could be heard as he came to the back of he queue joining on looking up the queue at luis standing there talking with his cousin mark who was only one year older than him leroy was three years older than luis

I got my hot water cuz,mark said looking up the queue at leroy who was now walking up the queue towards him with no intentions of waiting in an ordely manner in line barging pass all the other inmates until he stood right beside mark and luis

then leroy could hear mark say loudly with a laugh

hay what's up cuz ?

leroy then said,whats up cuz ?

do you like fish leroy ?

leroy looked at mark with a puzzled expression on his face standing there looking at mark holding his hot cup of coffee in one hand

as luis started pouring some hot water from the urn into his plastic mug his ears listening to mark and leroy

what kind of question is that leroy asked ?

I said do you like fish he askked again ?

yes of course I do leroy answered

mark then laughed aloud saying well there's a place at the back of the queue

they both started laughing together luis turned around with his cup filled with hot water getting the joke then laughed on with them leroy had already jumped the queue taking his turn now at the urn ignoring all the other inmates waiting in the queue

mark and luis waited by the urn for leroy to finish filling his mug with hot water

then leroy said where we going boys

lets take our seats in the tv room,mark said

they all walked off on through the ground floor to the tv room following him all dressed in their blue jeans with prison blue t-shirt

they walked into the tv room behind a few other inmates then each took a seat in the middle of the back row the last row right at the back

you know what cuz,leroy said,sitting down next to mark

luis sat next to leroy who was sitting in the middle of them

whats that mark asked leaning forward putting his plastic blue mug down on the floor near his feet leaning back up putting his hand into his jeans pocket taking out his packet of tobacco

I got given a new job today i'm working in the laundry factory cuz,I started this afternnon then took a sip of his hot tea placing it then on his lap still holding on to the big plastic yellow handle

Mark looked to his left at leroy while luis looked to his right

thats good news mark replied,im glad for you cuz

yes nice one bruv,luis said

yeah thanks guys also guess what leroy continued to say,im working with one of francis friends so he had better watch his back,leroy said then laughed

any news from the pison officers cuz about the cell transfer

mark had now put tobacco into some of his rolling paper he had taken out from his packet of rolling papers which he had taken out of his tobacco pouch now rolling it up between his fingers

leroy took another sip of his tea which was boiling hot in his mug

I'm still waiting for the prison officer to let me know if I will get transfered I did say this morning I will know sometime this evening,mark replied bringing the roll up to his lips licking it from end to end sticking it together leaving the tobacco pouch with the rolling papers on his lap

anyone got a light,he said

yeah luis said taking out a box of matches from his jeans pocket

hand these to mark bruv,he said to leroy

let me make one cuz,leroy asked as he took the matches giving them to mark

mark held the roll up in his mouth between his lips opening the match box taking out a match which had been split right down the middle into two pieces he took one half slim match out from the matchbox then struck it watching it light the roll up in his mouth lighting it then brought the lighten match to the roll up in his mouth lighting it drawing in his roll up taking a deep pull before outng the match dropping it to the floor by his feet

yeah make one mark said,picking up his pouch with papers handing them to Leroy with the matches

leroy got your matches luis okay

yeah bruv,no problem luis replied,leroy started making himself a roll up

luis sat there sipping on his mug of coffee looking ahead of him at the rows of wooden chairs slowly filling up with inmates still coming into the tv room secretively he was watching out with his mates just to see their sorrowfull faces knowing now the game had changed knowing his life was no more at fret he was no more being hunted no more the innocent prey waiting to be eaten up by the pack of wolves because now he was being protected by wild lions

the kings of the iron jungle and he also knew it and there was nothing he could do about it unless he wanted his head ripped right off his shoulders with his weak followers

he took his tobacco out of his other jeans pocket

luis have one of marks,leroy said,seeing what luis was about to do yeah luis have one of mine mark responded taking another pull on his roll up then reached acrosss to the empty chair picking up his blue plastic mug of coffee taking his first sip while holding the half smoked roll up in his other hand

then smiled saying look who just walked in to leroy and luis it was francis with one of his trouble making mates

francis walked to the middle row of the one hundred rows of chairs with his friend they both took their seats

leroy passed the pouch to luis with the papers and matches

give me a light cuz,before you finish your roll

mark stayed silent while holding the roll up in between his fingers then leaned his hand forward towardss leroys face

leroy brought his face towards marks roll up holding his roll up in his mouth with his lips then allowed the end of his roll up to touch the end of marks smoking roll up by sucking on his own roll up he got a light

saving the matches in luis match box more than wasting another match away which always came in very useful in the prison system especially at night times when you were locked away in your cell you would always be needing a more than enough and couldn't afford to run out leroy already knew all the procedures

don't worry guys I got my eyes on them leroy said sitting there in the middle taking a few quick pulls on his roll up to make sure it stayed alite while still holding one hand on his plastic mug luis had finished his roll up holding it in between his lips while he started tucking his tobacco pouch back into his jeans pocket

here you are luis,leroy said,holding his hand out to luis direction save your matches man

okay luis said pushing the pouch deep into his pocket then leaned toward leroys direction taking leroys roll up from out of his fingers getting himself a quick light

okay thanks,he said handing leroy back his roll up.

The light in the tv room was now turned off by one of the two prison officers standing at the entrance of the tv rooms double doors everyone was settling themselves down to watch the evening progrramme in the tv room while some spoke on quietly

20 minutes down the time line francis got up from his chair then walked pass the few wooden chairs to the end of his row then walked towards the double doors in the dim tv room pass the prison officers then left the tv room

leroy noticed him walking towards the door then leaving

I will be back now boys,he said after waiting for about two minutes to pass by getting up squeezing pass luis who didn't notice francis leaving the room

mark had seen francis leaving knowing also what leroy was up to or hoping to do,

he just kept his gaze forward watching the tv after leroy left the tv room mark sat on leroys chair next to luis saying then in a low voice I think leroy's gone out on a mission he's just followed francis friend out of the tv room

is that so bruv you reckon,luis replied.

leroy stepped out onto the ground floor landing he scanned all around to his left and right then looked up towards the landings above on landing one two and three where he could see one or two inmates on the landings but they were not the person he was looking for he started to walk the ground floor landing leading towards the pool table then notice francis standing next to the other friend who was siting down on one of the few wooden chairs near the pool table the friend who was in the tv room earlier was standing up talking to his mate,leroy slowly walked on pass continuing walking onwards to the toilet just a little further up ahead to the left al-right,he thought there will be more oppurtunitites its all just a matter of time with patience also good timing,he said to himself walking into the toilet even though he didn't need to use the toilet so he just walked up to the wash basin turning on the cold water tap starting to splash colds water onto his face,he then looked up at the large mirror just over the wash basin at his reflection in the mirror giving himself a smile inspecting himself his healthy looking round face with his slim mouthstache with black hair underneath his chin

you still got it son he could hear himself saying,the girls are still out there waiting for you,he smiled at himself again then turned off the cold water tap straightening himself out before he walked back out of the toilet looking first to the right towards the iron staircase,he was now walking up the ironstairs quickly looking to his left seeing several inmates sitting down near the poor table some playing on the wooden top football table others playing pool,his eyes were now in search out for the prison officers on the wing,he could see two at the far left of the ground floor landing there was another one standing near the outside door of the tv room talking to a inmate,up above on the landing he couldn't detect no white shirts so he quickly moved on forward to the iron staircase on his right

watching francis climb the stairs to the landing

he must be going to his cell to get something leroy started to think while his feet scaled the steps on the iron staircase swiftly getting onto francis's landing then watched francis dis-appear into his cell I hope he's all on his own leroy started to think approaching his cell,he could feel his blood starting to pump itself in his veins circulating around the whole of his body his heart starting to pump up and down loudly in his chest while his breathing sped up adrenaline,he thought,then smileds to himself pushing francis cell door open then stepped looked around seeing leroy standing inside of his cell hay dude what you doing in my cell,he said watching leroy push the cell door a little near to closed behind him

leroy stood there for a few seconds just looking at him

I said what are you doing in my cell man?

I just come to warn you,leroy then said,standing by the cell door

warn me about what I ain't done you nothing?

you and your mates have ben bully my mate luis,leroy said stepping now further into the cell

I don't know what your talking about dude he said stepping back further into his cell

I know what i'm talking about I was right there that night you lot ganged up against him

leroy said walking straight to give him a hard vicious punch right on his nose watching blood instantly running from his nose down to his lips

leroy threw a few more punches which landed directly on francis left jaw and right jaw before giving him a uppercut punch right underneath his chin driving his fist hard upwards lifting francis heads backwards before leroy stepped a little backward watching his victim slump down on to his knees unconscious as he was bending down on his cell floor leroy watched as francis slumped to the cell floor,thats for luis he said before turning around walking to the cell door opening it stepping out onto the landing having a quick look around on the landing as he closed the cell door shut locked then slowly made his way down the landing down the ironstairs walking through the ground floor landing pass the inmates being entertained by their games looking at the other of francis friend who was now playing pool before walking on towards the TV room like he hadn't done anything wrong.

CHAPTER
77   CRUISING

Carlos his car was just taking a right turn off the north circular turning into Palmers Green the area where luis lived,he looked to his left at luis fast asleep in the passenger seat while he drove on only a few minutes now away from luis flat as the artist *Bob Marley* sang away singing *Jamming* he arrived at luis street then pulled his car up right outside luis flat.

luis had been asleep for some time he had been sleeping most of the journey back since carlos left bristol connecting back up onto the M4 motorway to london,it didn't take carlos very long because the M4 was quiet concerning traffic, just what he liked,it was a very smooth straight forward journey back to london,now he had just pulled up his handbrake turning his music volume down then put his gear in neutral keeping his engine ticking over

he said leaning over to his left giving luis a little shove

hay luis your home mate

uumm,yes what did you say he mumbled

I said we are back in london i'm outside your's

what already that was quick,luis said with his eyes now opened looking very tired

recognising while noticing he was right outside of his flat

that was quick,bruv,he continued saying as he started undoing his seatbelt

my rucksack man and my jacket

your jacket is on the back seat I will open the boot for you,your rucksack is in the boot to

okay luis said looking back to Carlos

yeah nice one bruv,he said stretchnig his fist out towards his good friend then the both of them spudded each other

carlos pressed a buton just below his steering wheel hearing the boot unlock as luis got out the car shutting the passenger door then opened the back door on his side of the car leaned himself in pulled out his jacket then got out closing the door behind him,then went to the boot opened it up stood by the boot putting on his jacket then took out his green rucksack and a plastic bag which had his share of magic mushroom inside of it,he then closed the boot walkled to carlos side of the car tapped on carlos drive side front window

carlos looked up at,then winded down the window to its halfway mark

I will phone you tomorrow luis said,then smiled at him holding his plastic bag up in the air infront of his face while having the rucksack secured through one of his arms around his shoulder

hay bruv if anything if you are going to try those magic mushrooms you got in your plastic bag don't take no more than forty

they will take you on a trip into another world trust me bruv,he said,before turning around walking off to his flats entry.

CHAPTER 78
PLODDING ON

The earthly worldly time clock was steadily moving it's time forward through the days of the week turning the weeks into months,spring summer with autum had used up all of their moving days the Winter season was now upon us,novemmber had used up all of it's days the days date was now the 1st december,most people now had christmas on their minds for this was the next big celebrating festive,people sneakily buying their little presents here and there for their little growing children with their teenage sons and daughters,hiding them away in secret places in their homes until christmas morning.

Although it was the winter season the climate this year for winter 2019 december was not yet bitter cold even this morning on the 1st december the sun could be seen glowing up there in the light blue sky where bit and pieces of white clouds could be notice slowly drifting through the clear sky,the weather was unpredictable,it was only a few days ago the early morning came with cold frost on all the roof tops of the houses with buildings in london city witrh rainy mornings wet afternoons and very cold evenings,if you didn't check the weather report today you would say to yourself we may not see a single rain drop today the way the morning had started.

.   Stephen was up in his flat this morning having left his bed around 9am,going imto the kitchen putting water in the kettle turning it on while he wandered off to the bathroom to wash his face and brush his teeth,he was on his own as usual unless he was at Sarina's home,he was surprised when he climbed out from his bed then opened the curtains to see the golden sun outside this morning glowing in the blue heavenly sky.

Now back in london he had been in his flat on his own all day today and yesterday working again on his writing projec,tapping away constantly on his keyboard,world of words plucking them from his minds thoughts putting them together into sentences turning them into new chapters.

He had phone sarina yesterday speaking with her telling her he would come and spend some time with her tomorrow,he had brought her to alex's flat last christmas the both of them staying there in Bristol until the New Year but Sarina had not been to Wales as yet

soon babes,he told her on the phone,soon

after he had finished in the bathroom,he walked back into the kitchen to finish making himself a cup of coffee,he had made his mind up from last night he wouldn't be at home tapping away all day on his keyboard today because he was pleased with himself with the amount of typing he had done since starting this novel the begining of October 2019.

CHAPTER
79   RELAXING

The time of this new day had now pushed itself forward through the midday the morning glowing sun was lasting it had not faded neither had it disappeared it was still up there glowing but the heat of its bright rays couldn't be felt on the skin the air wasn't warm either even though the sun was out willing to show its face this afternoon.

You could hear the sound of a mobile phone ringing away in the bedroom of the one bedroom flat,a naked arm moved itself fumbling around on top ofthe duevet in search of the ringing phone without moving their head from off the pillow believing they had a good idea of where on the bed the phone as their hand keep feeling and searching away the phone kept ringing until the head ofthe person raised itself up giving up now on the blind search looking on top of the duvet where the mobile phone was as they spotted the phone with their tired looking face with sleepy eyes reaching for it the mobile stopped ringing away you could hear the voice of the person say in the fairly dark bedroom where the curtains were still closed a hand now held onto the phone as they laid back down their head on the pillow feeling the tiredness of sleep still near to them,they brought the phone to their face looking to see who the caller was

mm,no name they said in their thoughts just a number

laying there with their head on the pillow looking at the number on the screen

I don't know who's number this is the person thought as their finger pressed onto the return button

laying there with their head on the pillow phone infront of their face looking at the number they had just pressed ringing then they pressed the loud speaker button then let go of his mobile phone leaving it there resting infront him waiting to see who the caller was the phone connected straight away a loud voice came over the phone

alright luis how are you

hi ok bruv,who is this luis said laying there not moving his head

from his pillow but just looking at the phone by his face next to the pillow on the duvet

its me curtis did you guys get back to london okay

yes bruv we got back okay i'm going to have to store your name in my phone I forgot to do it when i was down in Port Talbot yesterday,I have got your number but I didn't know who was calling me luis said still laying there not moving

okay well we are going to have to arrange a day when I can come up and buy some stuff of you guys ok i'm really interested boyo,once ive gotten rid of what iv'e got here i'm going to call you straight away I will have the cash ready I won't let you guys down curtis sounded very keen on the phone luis thought

as he was saying to curtis hay bruv don't worry there's no big rush just call me when you want to reload then we will get together to do some good business okay

alright luis no problem boyo,don't forget to store my number alright will call you soon

the next thing the phone cut off

luis shook head while still laying his head on his pillow then laughed again,crazy,he thought to himself.

CHAPTER 80
TIME MOVES

Throughout the passing new week stephen spent the next few days at sarina's home with her two children then picked up his son jaydon on the friday morning going then back over to Sarina's where they all spent the weekend together,he spoke with his brother alex and mark throughout that passing time also his sister lucy and jean,his siter christine phoned him asking him when he was going to pass around and pay her a visit,

I may come if I find the time this week,sis,he said but i'm not promising anything,if I do I will bring your nephew jaydon with me,but it doidn't happen,stephen spent the whole rest of the weekend with sarina her two children and jaydon.

CHAPTER 81   AT
LUIS HOME

Luis and carlos had a crazy week that same week,carlos driving over to luis on the thursday the day after they had gotten back to london from port talbot luis urging carlos to take some magic mushrooms with him just take forty each and we will trip together luis urged

as carlos sat there on the sofa in the living room

come on carlos,luis said,standing there infront of him with eighty magic mushrooms he had already counted separated even had washed that early evening

it's different from anything iv'e ever taken in my life,he told carlos,they are amazing bruv

luis had told carlos earlier about how he felt the other day when he had taken them for the first time ever in port talbot while he was sitting in his sofa in his green tracksuit bottoms with slippers on his feet with a light green t-shirt on,carlos sitting next to him

I went into a totally different world bruv,its not easy to explain but everything just changed around me bruv,even the people they all looked weird,he said as he thought of those moments laughing excitedly to himself,everyone I was looking at had different shape heads bruv with odd shaped bodies it was like I was in lego land crazy bruv,he told carlos who sat there listening with interest

hold on luis said,walking out of his living room then came

back a few seconds later from his bedroom with a plain A4 size peice of white paper with a lot of magic mushroom on which he then put onto his coffee table infront of carlos

looks like you've been preparing yourself carlos uttered,looking at the white sheet of paper with the magic mushrooms on them

yeah I washed those lot earlier and i've been drying them out in my bedroom by the radiator they look more a white colour now don't they

yeah they don't look dark anymore,carlos said taking a closer look at them on the white paper,picking one up with his fingers bringing it closer to his face

how many you got there? he asked luis

there's eighty there altogether,can't you see i've split them into two lots one lot for you and one lot for me bruv

carlos still held the one single mushroom inbetween his fingers

I don't know man,i'm driving ain't it and I don't know how they are going to affect me,if they mess with my head I won't be able to drive back to mines bruv

don't watch that luis replied,just chill here with me if anything you ain't doing nothing important today,it's not as though you got to go to work you muppet luis said then laughed,now standing in the middle of his living room just behind the coffe table

so what your saying then bruv,luis asked

you know what carlos said,there goes my first one putting the magic mushrroom he was holding in his fingers straight into his mouth then swallowed it,okay thirty nine more to go then bruv,leaning forward in the sofa towards the coffee table picking up another one putting it into his mouth as luis watched him eating mushroom number two let me get you a glass of coke and get myself one also its easier to grab a mouth full then wash them down bruv

luis left the living room going into his kitchen coming back moments later with two glasses of coke drinks in his hand

here you are bruv he said,putting one of the glasses on the coffee table for carlos

then started taking some of the mushrooms from his half on the white paper putting them into his mouth until he had half a mouth full of magic mushrooms washing them down with a mouth full of coke,they don't taste very nice though he said after swallowing his first half

carlos now had his mouth half filled with magic mushrooms,he half backed his glass of coke in his mouth washing down the mushrooms,then went for his last load on the sheet of paper

luis had already taken all his magic mushrooms up and was loading the last few into his mouth while he watched carlos picking up his mushrooms popping them into his mouth in small bunches of five and more until the paper had no more mushrooms on it

alright then luis said with his mouth now half full with magic mushrooms holding his glass with half the amount of coke left inside of it

carlos looked towards luis

    luis came towards carlos stretchewd his glass out tapped it onto carlos

cheers bruv,

then the both of them washed their half filled mouths of magic mushrooms down with the coke in their glasses

alright thats that then carlos said still sitting on the sofa looking up at luis standing near infront of him,then put his glass on the table

yeah it takes about half and hour up to one hour before you start tripping bruv,fasten your mental seatbelt bruv and get ready for the ride of your life laugh luis feeling a little nervous for he didn't really know what to really expect this time,even though he had already experienced one trip

I tell you what lets go get a couple of can of lager from the off-licence we might as well luis asked

okay carlos replied,

luis put his glass on the table

give me a few minutes to get my trainers and jacket on bruv luis said before wandering out of the living room into his hall-way to put his trainers and jacket on

you ready carlos

yeah bruv carlos said getting up leaving the sofa's comforts slowly walking out of the living room into the hallway where luis was waiting for him by his front door luis opened his door walked out onto his driveways path

just shut it behind you bruv,

yeah no problem carlos answered ,walking out from the flat shutting the door behind him.

The off-licence was no more than a five minute walk away from luis flat the both of them bought a few cans of lager

carlos bought a packet of cigarettes with a few snacks then they both walked back to the flat.

Now there the two of them sat in the living room,carlos back on the sofa he sat on earlier,luis sat on a single arm-chair on the opposite side of the living room from him.they had the tv on with the games console out playing the play station together while drinking a can of lager each they had another six more cans there on the coffee table between them, carlos was inbetween munching on a packet of crisp when all of a sudden he let out a big loud scream

whats the matter,luis looked quickly then said as carlos got up from the sofa,dropping the games console controls onto the sofa

what,s the matter with your head man,he said looking at luis with wide open staring eyes like he was looking at something aweful

nothing man what your talking about bruv,luis questioned

your heads tiny bruv it's shrunk,whats happened to you luis

luis laughed saying your starting to trip bruv,looking at carlos staring at him strangely as he walked forward knocking the opened can of lager he had put on the carpet near to his feet over spilling it all out onto the carpet

look what you've done now you have spilt your drink all over my carpet bruv,

carlos didn't pay any attention to what luis had just said,he just stood there in his spot staring at luis while the lager kept pouring out onto the carpet

your head luis your head carlos shouted again,its growing it's getting bigger now

luis got up laughed at arlos as he picked up the spilt can then quickly walked out into the kitchen dumping it into the kitchen bin,he was still laughing walking away into the kitchen saying carlos your tripping man,it's all just an illusion,walking back into the living room

seeing carlos kneeling down dipping his finger into the spilt lager on the carpet

then looking at luis with the dread of fear on his face thats my blood bruv,iv'e cut myself bruv what your talking about it's the lager you just spilt on my carpet

why are you lying to me,carlos replied angrily,i'm not stupid its my blood im cut man he said,pulling his jumper and t-shirt up showing his bare skin

see i'm bleeding man showing luis nothing but his pale skinned stomach

how did I cut myself,my blood is all over your carpet bruv

luis laughed even more at the crazy behaviour of his friend

sit down carlos and relax bruv,there's not cut there believe me man,calm down it's the mushrooms bruv,your just having a bad trip

alright carlos said,pulling back down his clothes sitting back down now trying to get a grip of himself,your heads massive bruv and you got hairy lips bruv,

luis couldn't help himself but to laugh again by hearing what carlos just said

I told you bruv,fasten your mental seatbelt your going on the ride of your life he said,standing there infront of carlos who seem to be having a bad trip while luis laughed on and on seeming to be having a good trip this time around.

CHAPTER 82
PORTUGAL CAFE

Throughout that week luis and carlos took a few more magic mushroom trips tripping their minds off having good with bad experiences they both laughed at times until their stomachs ached on many occasions for hours through the days,they even boiled up some of the mushrooms in a sauce pan of water at carlos flat turning them into mushroom juice drinking the juice,even giving some of the mushroom's juices to some of their friends the both of them laughing together while tripping off the mushroom,laughing at their mates who were now going on a strange mental journey of their minds experiencing things odd,bizzarre and weird seeing all different kinds of illusion's also feeling all types of weird feelings.

Now they had used up all the magic mushrooms they had picked together which had lasted them nearly 2 weeks,knowing now their tripping days on the mushrooms had come to its end,already knowing they were lucky to pick what they had picked what they had picked at the time when they were in port talbot because they were there picking at the end of the magic mushroom season,they would now have to wait until autumn next year now to get their crazy magic mushroom kicks again.

Luis was out today this afternoon he was on the way to edmonton to the area where his mother's shops was the Portgul Cafe,right now he was waiting at the bus stop for his bus,he had on his thick black winter jacket,black woolly hat with a scarf around his neck,the air was cold today which was blowing through the air the concrete roads with pavements were wet with the early morning with early afternoon falling rains although the rains had now stopped you had to make sure you were dressed proper for the cold miserable temperature.

Luis stood there at the bus stop with a few other people waiting,he didn't wait very long only 1 minute before the bus came,on he got with a few other people,he tapped his plastic oystercard on the digital device system which then showed the bus driver luis had enough money on his oystercard to travel,he walked on up the stairs of the red double decker bus passing a few passenger sitting down in the upstairs seats taking himself a seat at the left side back of the bus.

It was only a 15 minute bus ride to edmonton to the main street called fore street to his mums cafe,his mother had phone him on his mobile phone this morning asking him if he could pass by the cafe this afternoon if he weren't busy,to help her move some old junk which was in the store room at the back of the cafe which was taking up space for to long ,she needed the space for other reasons,his stepdad would be at the cafe with his old van parked at the back of the cafe waiting for him to help out.

As luis was on his journey there his mobile phone in his winter jacket started ringing,he pulled it out looked at who was calling him,it was curtis,he answered it

hi you okay curtis he said holding the phone to his ears

yes you alright luis,I need to buy some cocaine from you boy-o,all my stuff has run down low,i'm on my last few sales when can we meet up he said down the phone

okay I hear you curtis give me two or three hours then I will get back to you with all the information,make sure your phone is on okay no problem boyo curtis replied before then phone went silent

luis puit the mobile phone back inside his jacket pocket continuing on his journey to his mum's cafe.

The bus stopped at the stop he needed to get off, he was soon down the steps walking out of the bus crossing the busy road fore street walking to the Portugal Cafe,walking in through the cafe door pass the few tables and chairs,in the front of the cafe there were a few customers eating their afternoon meals while watching the flat screen tv attached top the cafe wall.

His mum was at the counter serving a customer handing them some change.

Hi luis go to the back please he's waiting for you

okay mum,he said then he walked through the entry while undoing the buttons on his jacket walking pass the entry taking off his jacket walking further into the back of the cafe to see his stepdad

ho so you are hear then,his stepdad said seeing luis walk into the storeroom he was standing in holding a old stainless steel sink unit in his arms

help me with this,he said to luis

ok i'm just going to put my jacket here in the cloakroom were they all kept their jackets coats and bags,he put his jacket and scarf inside there then went to help his stepdad move the sink through the back of the cafe into the back lane where his stepdads van was,the back door of the van was already opened,luis held onto one end of the sink,his stepdad held onto the other end,

he could see as he got closer to the van other bits with pieces of waste in the back,pieces of old metals,with pieces of wood mixed in with a bit of rubble,they chucked the old sink into the back of the van then walked back into the back garden of the cafe then back into the cafe to get rid of the rest of the old junk,after removing all of the rubbish.

Luis told his mother he was going with his stepdad for a drive to the rubbish dump leaving his jacket in the store room he jumped into the old van driving off down the back lane onto the main road following the traffic flow out of edmonton,his stepdad driving the few miles to enfield town where they emptied the back of the vans contents into a large legal dumping area then drove back to the cafe where luis stayed for a little time talking to his mother and stepdad.

CHAPTER
83   WAITING

The price for the fuel is £25 sir

he took his contactless visa debit card out from his wallet,swiped it across the paying device in the petrol station

here is your receipt sir

he took the receipt left the service station walking over to his motorbike put his helmet over his head turned on his ignition pulled in the clutch,reeved it flicking it into gear slowly letting go of the clutch then off he rode joining up with the traffic on the Neath road a few miles away from port talbot.

His mind was on business,he was hoping to get that call back hopefully in the next hour or so,if he did then he would enjoy a nice long ride out of his little country town to the big old smoke london city,he hadn't been there for years infact he had only been there once decades ago in his junior school days on a junior school trip when he was only 10 years old with all his classmates they all went to the Madam Tussaud in Baker Street then to the West End for a day trip,the only thing he could remember when he was at the West End were pairs of legs thousands of pairs of legs hundreds of pairs of legs thousands of pairs of legs of people walking every where just legs peoples legs,he must of been that small for it was the only memory which filled his mind of london apart from going on a small little underground trains which moved fast and speedily witrh small strange looking automatic doors that opened and closed on their own,london,he thought as he rode on down Briton ferry towards Baglan,well it wont be legs I be seeing this time if I go there because i'm a big boy now I will be able to see what the big city looks like this time.

A short time later he was outside his home parking up his bike in his front drive then went into his home closing his front door taking off his leather bike jacket leaving it on the sofa in his front room putting his front door keys with his bike keys on his mantel piece with his mobile phone then turned on his tv then sat on his sofa holding the tv remote control in his hand,he sat there flicking through the channels

mm,nothing much on he left the tv on the game show programme called The Chase,sitting back watching it,a few minutes later his mobile started ringing on top of the mantel piece,putting the remote control on the sofa next to his leather jacket feeling excited saying to himself getting up

this is the call i've been waiting for,quickly picking it up answering it without even looking who the caller was with a big happy smile on his face from ear to ear

yeah is that you luis ?

no it's bulla

ho sorry I thought you was someone else sorry bulla boyo,curtis said,his tone of voice changed

how are you bulla

i'm cool man I was just wondering when are you going to reload

well ,well i've been busy I was going to but something new has come up curtis said,nervously down the phone not being to sure how to answer bulla's simple question,because he had not made up his mind as yet how he was going to break the news to bulla that he was no longer going to buy from him and the dread ,he wasn't going to tell him he met luis in his town and was going to start doing business with him but he realised he had just slipped up by calling bulla by luis name,he was hoping now bulla didn't catch on

bulla then asked him,when he was going to be to buy his next load

soon bulla soon,i've nearly finished what i've got here I will call you back in a day or two ok

alright bulla said then dis-connected the call from curtis leaving curtis standing by his mantel piece staring down now at his mobile phone in his hand.

CHAPTER 84
WONDERING

Just a few presses on the numbers on his mobile phone a little few moments of waiting before the voice of the dread was heard

alright bulla,whats up man,

yeah cool dread,I just came off the phone just now to curtis,he says's he's not ready to buy anything from us yet,he's telling me he ain't finished shifting his last load,saying he will get back to me in a few days

yeah I hear you bulla,thats no problem

bulla then said sitting there in his car in cardiff city 19 miles away from bridgend town where the dread was

I got some instinct going on here with me,I think curtis is up to something suspicious

what do you mean? the dread asked as he also sat in his car which was parked in the car park of the Trump pub carpark in brigend town centre

as soon as he came on the phone he started acting a bit suspicios man,it wasn't like him and you know what bulla then said

whats that? the dread asked

the first thing he said when he answered my call was luis,he called me luis,I told him i'm not luis,it's me bulla

mm,bulla could hear the dread say,then the dread said thats a bit odd man does curtis know luis

I don't know bulla replied pressing the loud speaker button on his mobile phone then placed the phone on his lap

so how would he know luis then,maybe he's talking about a different luis,the dread stated

yeah I know what you are saying dread,but it was the way he started to sound after mentioning the name luis he seemed really nervous after that,something is up dread i'm telling you

mm,the dread said sitting there holding his mobile to the side of his head while his free hand held onto a bunch of his dread-locks feeling the size of the bunch in his palm squeezing softly on them

hay you know what bulla,i'm wondering if he know's mark?

I wouldn't know I don't know curtis that well bulla answered

well in that town nearly everyone know's mark bird and the bird family,the dread said,leaving his locks to fall onto his lap raising his hand up to his black glassess shifting it a little on the bridge of his nose bulla don't forget luis know's mark

they were in prison together a few years back and it's mark that got you to know luis maybe when he came down to give us the gear last time he went down to visit mark in port talbot it's only a 30 minute drive from your area

yeah bulla said,thats possible but where does curtis come into the equation bulla asked

thats for you and me to find out the dread answered

mm,I suppose so,he could hear bulla say

dread just think if it's the real luis he mentioned to me on the phone and has started doing business with him that means me and you are out of the picture there's no more middle man no more quick easy money bulla felt angry in hearing the words of his own mouth right now he was feel really annoyed really vexed with curtis

alright i'm not going to be hanging around talking to you about this on the phone dread i,m going to phone luis right now and trick him into telling me he knows curtis and if he does know him then what i'm feeling is right and real

ok i will leave you to it bulla,get back to me and let me know if luis know's him or not

ok dread call you soon if anything ok

no problem the dread said before they both dis-connected

as bulla sat there behind his steering wheel in his driver seat,he scrolled to the contact part of his mobile phone then scrolled up until the name luis appeared then pressed the call symbol allowing the phone to ring.

CHAPTER
85   DEBATING

Back in the North of london a little earlier 5 minutes ago while bulla was on his mobile phone talking to the dread,back at his home in Palmers Green luis was also on his mobile phone talking to curtis he had not long firstly spoke with his main dealer named mario asking him if he could deliver 3oz of cocaine to his home tonight because he had a buyer who maybe coming up london to buy it tomorrow or the day after

yes I will drop it around tonight mario told him,then dis-connected the call luis then phoned curtis telling him he would be getting the goods tonight and that he could come and pick up the goods anytime that suited him

curtis then telling luis he would be riding his motorbike up to london to meet him sometime tomorrow afternoon or early evening but would confirm the times with him properly later tonight

no problem,luis said before ending the call

,moments later luis phone started ringing again,while he sat there relaxed on his living room's sofa,he picked his mobile up from the sofa thinking who is this

looking at the name ho,it's,bulla,so he answered the call straight away

hay you alright bulla what can I do for you bruv

yes you alright luis my brother,I just need to ask you a question

whats that,a question ? luis asked

yeah luis i've not long come off the phone to a guy in port talbot called curtis do you know him?

luis,sat there on his sofa listening then answered

well I don't know him exactly i've only just met him the other week in port talbot when I was visiting mark bird after I drop off some stuff to you.

you know mark ?

of course I know mark,he's my ex cell mate a good friend of mine,it's mark that introduced me to you remember bulla stated sitting there in his car

yeah bruv I know that so what's your problem?

my problem is you are cutting me out of business if you are going to be trading your coke to curtis because we buy off you and trade it to him, you get me

luis got up from his sofa then started slowly walking around his living room then said to bulla,bruv it's not my problem it's business bruv

if you are willing to travel up here to london to collect the goods from me then the business still stands between us but if curtis is willing to travel to get his stuff from me direct,it saves me time and my friend travelling all the way to cardiff to deliver it to you,curtis is coming up to collect his goods from me some time tomorrow afternoon or evening if he is willing to travel it saves me time bruv and time is business so what you got to say about that

bulla sat there listening

I hear you luis,ok if I need anything I got your number ok

alright bulla next time bruv,luis said,then ended the call

luis sat back down in his sofa placing his mobile phone by his side he sat there thinking for a moment then picked back up his mobile phone scrolled to curtis's name called it then waited.

CHAPTER 86
INFORMATION

The dread just shut his car door locked it then walked on up his pathway opening then closing the driveway gate behind him

he opened his front door stepped inside his home closing his front door

it's me babes he shouted in the hallway then walked into the kitchen getting a clean drinking glass from the kitchen cupboard opened the fridge taking out a bottle of coke then walked just a few steps to the kitchen table where he put his glass filling the pint glass right up to the brim then screwed back on the coke top walking back to the fridge putting the bottle back inside then closing the fridge door,opening then the fridge freezer part of the fridge pulling out the ice tray taking the tray over to the sink,putting his glasss of coke on the sink unit then popped six square ice cubes into the glass as his mobile in his jeans pocket started ringing.

He quickly rushed back to the fridge putting the ice tray back inside as his phone continued to ring shut the freezer door then took his mobile phone from out of his jeans pocket answering it

Yeah dread's speaking,he said

yeah dread I just came off the phone to the luis,I was right about curtis he's going to be doing business direct with luis the both of them did meet up a few weeks ago the time he came down to give me the goods the dread listened on,picking up his glass of coke with ice from the sink unit then took a seat at the kitchen table

damn it the dread said,that,s our bread and butter gone from that link now

he will still do the busines with us and cut curtis out only if we are willing to do the travel up to london to collect the goods because curtis is willing to travel to collect saving him time travels he told me

ah it's a long thing man,for the small rewards it's not worth the trouble travelling with all that amount of drugs bulla,you get me

yeah bulla replied,sitting there in his drivers seat

curtis is going up to london tomorrow,bulla continued,he's really slapped me in my face dread,he's not going to get away with this,trust me man

it's like he has stolen my contact and I need the easy cash

hay Bulla cool down man,it's not the end of the world,you win some you lose some

yeah dread,well this pone i'm not going to lose

look here bulla don't worry yourself and don't do anything stupid there will be plenty more business coming your way and my way to,alright dread I just called to let you know ok

hay bulla remember I got rid of 1 ounces down here last time so don't mess up things with luis becasuse I may need his goods one day soon remember this okay

yeah dread,bulla said before he ended the call

the dread put his mobile phone on the kitchen table then took a nice big sip of his glass of cold coke.

CHAPTER 87 BULLA

As bulla sat there in his car luis sat there with the mobile phone to his ears hearing it ringing until Curtis answered

alright curtis,I had to ring you back bruv

okay is everything alright,curtis asked

yeah every things cool regarding business,its just that I just got a phone call from your ex dealer bulla asking me how did I know you with all the rest of it,I just told him the truth bruv because I got nothing to hide and neither have you I ain't robbing no-one

okay luis,curtis spoke

I don't think he will be pleased me getting it directly from you,I haven't told him yet curtis said sitting there in his front room next to his bike leather jacket,

he was glad luis had called him telling him bulla was snooping around but also surprised that bulla had caught on so quickly realising what he was up to,all because of that one little slip up of his lips,he thought by calling him luis name

and yes your right,you aint robbing no one neither have I,well i'm going to call him and set the record straight luis

okay curtis,let me know when you can about what time you will be in london tomorrow then I will tell you where to me us

curtis got up from the sofa still holding onto his mobile phone walking out of his front room,I will tell you now he said I will be in london by 6pm walking down his hallway then turning right into his backroom of the house the door was already open walking into the room near to the far window as he spoke on

so where is the meeting point,

near the window there was a black wooden 3 draw chest of draws where he kept his papers and pens with other bits and pieces

have you got anything to write on ?luis asked

yes boyo,fire away,curtis said,opening the the top draw taking out a note pad with a pen standing there by the chest of draws placing the pad on top of it

luis then said,i'm giving you a postcode

okay i'm waiting replied curtis

hay curtis,you got that ?

yes got it,see you tomorrow 6pm any delays I will call you

okay luis said,before curtis phone went silent

curtis closed the notepad putting it back in the opened draw with the pen then closed the draw walking back out of the backroom holding his mobile phone walking through his hallway back to the front room taking his seat on the sofa again then called bullas number

bulla answered,saying curtis what's up man ?

I just need to talk to you bulla

bulla was still parked up in the same spot outside his home in his car

yeah I know what your up to bulla said,not giving curtis a chance to say what he was about to say

you are cutting me out of my own running man,don't worry about it everythings cool i've got a lot of other business on so it's cool okay bulla,curtis said it's just business man

yeah I know alright we will still keep in contact ok,don't lose my number okay,curtis said,then they both ended the call.

CHAPTER
88   REACHING

Bulla didn't waste no time sitting there in his driver seat as soon as he cut curtis from his phone he started pressing on a few numbers then pressed the loud speaker on his phone on his lap then waited

hi Ratchet you good man,he said loudly,

yeah bulla what's happening bro you good man,

okay I got some business lined up for you man

whats on the menu bro,anything tasty he asked

there will be a pay packet in it for you man,bulla replied

I want you to travel to port talbot with me tomorrow I will fill you in on more of the info later ok I will talk to you later okay

then bulla ended the call then phoned another number

alright blazer,how are you bro,he mentioned the same thing to blazer

yeah i'm interested bring me in on it he said

okay I will get back to you later bulla said,before dis-connecting.

CHAPTER 89

ON THE MOVE

The next day on the M4 motorway curtis rode on forward in the fast lane in top gear bobbing and weaving through the traffic his headlights were on shinning through the late afternoon darkness he knew he was ahead of time quickly looking at his small SATNAV device he attached to the front of his motorbike inbetween the steering wheel which had a little digital clock on the bottom right corner showing him the time was now 17.15pm.

He was dressed in motorbike black leather jacket with black leather padded trousers with black solid thick boots on his feet a black rucksack was securely fastened tightly strapped over his shoulders under his arms the rucksack which had money inside rested on his back speeding along glad to know it wasn't raining the motorway was dry which he certainly took advantage of turning up the reeves speeding on in top gear passing every single traffic infront of him carefully and everytime he saw the oppurtunity to pass them in the fast lane on their left or right if they ignored him flashing his headlights for them to move into the middle lane to allow him through.

He had left port talbot a little while ago the distance to

london from there was 177 miles his SATNAV told him he would arrive at the poscode he had put into it

at 17.45 he was just coming to the end of the M4 motorway follow the directions of his SATNAV into london among the busy traffic slowing down his speed keeping to the speed limit finding himself riding along the north circular carriageway.

He had spoken to luis on his mobile phone this morning,calling him telling him he would hopefully be at the postcode destination by 6pm

luis said no problem also to ring him once he had gotten there,

the postcode luis had given him was the postcode to his mother's cafe The Portugal Cafe.

Luis had spoke with carlos yesterday evening asking him if he could come to his flat in Palmers Green tomorrow afternoon letting him know curtis was to be coming early evening to collect,he wanted carlos to be there with him so he could carry the cocaine in Carlos's car meeting curtis outside his mother's cafe by car not having to use public transport,

carlos said he would be there at his flat tomorrow afternoon

he arrived there at 3.30pm luis opening his front door letting him into his flat,there they chilled out in his living room waiting for curtis's phone call.

Curtis arrived outside the cafe his SATNAV telling him you have arrived at your destination as he found himself riding up a busy high street which was Fore Street he slowed down his motorbike until it stoped,parking up dropping his feet to the ground looking all around seeing a lot of people of all nationalities walking pass him in both directions on the pavement black people white people all on the move he turned his ignition off pulling up his motorbike onto it's stand,sitting down on his bike seat pulling off his black helmet taking a look to his left and right sitting there realising he was parked right outside a small cafe which had a sign right across it saying The Portugal Cafe,he placed his helmet on the seat allowing it to rest on him unzipping his jacket taking his mobile phone out called luis number then waited for him to answer

hi luis i'm here at the postcode you gave me,I am right outside a cafe called The Portugal Cafe he said as luis voice came on his phone saying alright curtis

Okay thats good just go into the cafe and get yourself a drink or something to eat I will be with you in 15-20 minutes bruv

alright luis said then ended the call

he put his mobile phone back into the inside of his leather jacket pocket leaving it open then got off his motorbike undo-ing the SAT NAV removing it holding it in his hand then walked to the entrance of the cafe.

It was no more than 20 minutes before luis walked into the cafe seeing curtis sitting down at one of the cafe tables he sat right near the window near the cafe door en-trance with a plate of food infront of him eating away

carlos was parked up in his car at the back of the cafe waiting for them

alright curtis,luis said,seeing curtis sitting there eating up his food ,his rucksack was on the table

you hungry hay luis said,looking at curtis who smiled then nodded his head up and down at him with his mouth filled with food

luis took a seat next to him both their backs was towards the cafe window,luis looked down into the cafe between the few rows of tables which occupied a few customers who took up chairs eating and drinking,his mother was at the counter put-ting money into the till with her back towards him,luis kept his eyes on his mother as he spoke to curtis hoping while wait-ing for her to notice he was in the cafe,curtis didn't have any knowledge knowing it was luis mums cafe while he sat there filling his stomach with food

luis mum looked towards his direction noticing her son

luis put his hand up waving to her without saying a single word then turned his full attention back to curtis

take your time bruv,when you have finished eating we will go to the car it,s parked at the back of this cafe

okay curtis said as he started to clear up the rest of the food on his plate while luis now sat next to him tapping on a few digits on his mobile phone in his hand,yeah we wont be long he saids to carlos just a few minutes bruv then looked at curtis plate seeing he had nearly cleaned off all the food

luis dis-connected his phone got up walked over to the coun-ter had a few words with his mother while he waited for curtis to finish

okay mum love you,I will see you later he said before walking back to curtis who was now standing up grabbing hold of his rucksack looking towards luis walking towards his direction

come lets go luis said seeing curtis was ready.

CHAPTER 90 BULLA

All day yesterday evening also most of today bulla had been very busy on his mobile phone back and fro talking to ratchet and blazer he had arranged to pick them both up at separate times from their homes this evening then travel down to port talbot he didn't bother phone back Ryan the dread to let him know what he was up to since he had last spoken with him yesterday,he was on a mission now and not even the dread would be able to stop him neither change his mind,he was upset angry and filled with fury which was all directed towards curtis in having cut him out of the deal he had already set up with luis he couldn't believe it how things had suddenly changed so quick so unexpectedly he didn't see it coming it took him by surprise to see he was no longer earning quick easy cash,picking up from luis then delivering it to curtis now he felt curtis was dealing with him completely wrong and he wasn't having it he had been thinking to himself no way since he had last spoken with curtis yesterday ending their conversation politely ,now he was back inside of his car parked outside of his home with his mobile phone in his hand mind filled up with thoughts thinking about the late evening which laid ahead of him his eyes looking at the clock on his dashboard showing in the time was now 8.50pm.

CHAPTER 91 WAITING

The deal had been done the goods had been exchanged both parties were happy each getting what they wanted luis was back home in his flat and had been now for a few hours now, Carlos was also back home in South East london resting having not long gotten home parking his car up safetly outside his flat after spending atleast 2 hours at luis flat after giving the 3 ounces of cocaine to curtis at the back of the cafe in the back lane,curtis giving luis the cash,he didn't hang about for very long though ,luis asked him if he wanted to go to a winebar in the area for a quick one drink

no i'm okay curtis said I just want to get back to Port Talbot as he sat at the back of carlos car with his motorbike parked right behind carlos car

Now curtis had been riding on his motorbike in the distance of the late evening on the M4 motorway back to Wales with his black rucksack fastened tightly on his back carrying his cocaine he had already passed over the Seven bridge which separated England from Wales having rode past Gwent and Newport also Cardiff city he was only a 15 minutes journey away from port talbot.

While parked up in his street hidden out of the way in-between other parked cars bulla sat at the back of one of his friends car ratchets car who had met bulla at his home at this evening bringing along blazer who sat in the front passenger seat,changing their earlier plans of bulla coming to pick them both up deciding on using ratchets car for this evenings plans.

They had been waiting only 5 minutes having just got

to port talbot hoping they would get to curtis's street before him,bulla was hoping and praying his intentions was alright all the time he was sitting there in his car parked outside his home he had been thinking working out how long it would take curtis to get back to Port Talbot after picking up his drugs if he went there in the first place,he knew luis slipped up talking to him on the phone saying he and curtis had arranged to meet up in london 6pm so he had been calculating curtis's journey time hoping curtis wouldn't be staying in london for to long,he had worked it out that Curtis would or should arrive back in port talbot atleast inbetween certain hours to his calculations which were not far off from perfect,he was clever cunning also very crafty even though his two mates who sat in the car with him doubted his judgments,both saying how do you know if he has even gone to london he could of changed his mind making new arrangments with luis for another day even still he could be in london and not coming back straight away,his two mates felt they could be wasting their time they could be sitting in this street for hours even all night waiting for someone who might not even be turning up tonight,look bulla had told the both of them

trust me man I know what I am talking about as they drove into port talbot town through the streets to curtis street

park there he told ratchet

pointing to a space between two car on the otherside of the street from curtis home place then turned off his ignition

bulla pointed out Curtis's house for them

thats where he lives he said pointing out Curtis's home, well he's not home yet his house is in darkness thats a good sign so he must of done the journey to london bulla stated.

The street was quiet no one walked up and down it since they had parked up although a lot of the houses had their room lights on some upstairs some downstairs while a few other houses were in darkness to the street was very quiet

the three of them sat there ratchet and blazer were both wearing gloves on their hands it was another 10 minutes before
curtis motorbike rode into the street.

See I told you there he is bulla said watching him stopping his bike climbing off it while he kept the engine ticking over with his black rucksack fixed tightly on his back,he
walked a few steps to his small iron driveway gate opened it
then walked back to his motorbike jumped onto it then rode
slowly into his driveway all the time bulla and his two friends
watched on

okay get ready guys you know what to do don't leave the car
until he goes back to shut his gate so his back is towards you
when he's walking up his pathway to his front door

okay they both said watching on watching him,he parked his
bike pulling it up onto it's stand took the SATNAV off then
started walking back down his pathway as ratchet and blazer
had their hands on the car doors handle ready to open it

curtis shut is driveway gate

now bulla said,

the two car doors opened up,on the driver side ratchet and
blazer the both of them quickly ran across the road onto the
pavement straight to curtis's gate as his back was towards
them putting his keys into his frontdoor ratchet opened the
gate the both of them scrambled on through as Curtis turned
the key in his front door pushing his door open then turned
around to see who was that by his driveway gate

,before he knew it he was being pushed and shoved in through
his front door, the door closing behind him as he fell down
onto his hallway floor taking a few punches to his face in the
fairly dark hallway being lightened up by the light coming
through the square glass panel which made up the top quarter

of the front door.

Take that bag of your back now ratchet shouted holding curtis down to the carpeted hallway ground as curtis tried struggling to get back up onto his feet blazer kicked him hard in his side as the both of them struggled with him both punching him a few more times around his head and face, curtis screamed out blazer put his hand over curtis's mouth holding it there tightly to silence his shouts and screams as they both turned him over onto his stomach blazer still covering his mouth with his hand ratchet pulled a knife out from his side jacket pocket which he had hidden away then started cutting the straps on the rucksack until it fell from off curtis's back curtis curled himself up into a ball shape in his hallway feeling dazed and exhausted from all the struggling he had put up in his defence blood was dripping down from his nose he could taste the taste of blood in his mouth from a cut he could feel on the inside of his bottom lip.

While bulla sat at the back of ratchet's car outside waiting for them to get back to thje car, he could see from where he sat as he watched the both of his friends running across the road onto the pavement then in through curtis's front gate pushing curtis into his home closing his door behind him, bulla didn't expected them to be going into the house they were suppose to hold him up by his front door then grab the bags of drugs from him or threaten him to take his rucksack off,when he saw they had gone into curtis's house he thought well it's much more safer this way for no one will see what's happening,they had been in there about 1 minute now as bulla sat there looking all around out through the windows of the back of the car, the street was still empty,no one was around,they should be out soon he thought to himself with the bag of drugs.

Ratchet grabbed the rucksack off curtis back while he held onto his knife come on lets go he said,standing up holding the rucksack in his hand looking at blazer holding his hand around curtis's mouth,rachet punched curtis with a few more solid hard punches to his face as curtis laid on his stomach blazer got up and kicked curtis hard in his face knocking him completely out,they both left him unconscious on his hallway carpet before opening the front door walking out closing the front door behind them ratchet holding tightly onto the rucksack.

CHAPTER 92 ASHLEY

This early evening ashley had only just closed his flats home front door behind him turning on the downstairs hallway light,now he was standing in his hallway taking off his jacket putting it on the coat hanger before turning around looking at the pile of letters on the floor near the door at the bottom of the stairs,he kicked off both his shoes then slipped his both feet into his slippers waiting there for him at the bottom of the stairs,picking up the letters then made his way upstairs through his upstairs hallway walking straight into his dining room

aaww,that's where it is,he told himself looking at his mobile phone resting there on his three seater leather sofa,he had been worried all week having spent a week away at a friends of his home in Swansea city ,a nice long break from Port Talbot,he had taken a few days off work well in advance knowing now he would be back at his hair dresser shop on Forge Road next to Station Road early tomorrow morning.

He sat down next to his mobile phone putting all the letters right beside him then picked up his mobile pressing the on button

mm,his phone battery had completely run out and needed charging it was flat dead,getting up he could see the phone charger already plugged into the switch socket in his dining room wall near the rooms double glazing window not to far away from the tv plug,he walked over to it then connected the phone charger to his phone then left it there turned on his tv picked up the remote control from the top of his tv,dropping it onto his sofa before walking out of his dining room just a few feet away into the kitchen where he opened up the fridge taking out a small bottle of water from a six packet closing the fridge untwisting the plastic top as he walked back into the hallway,he felt good to be back home he felt relaxed.

Ashley lived alone having been separated from his long time girlfriend a little time ago,he had been living at this flat in Port Talbot in the sandfields estate area right near the beach 3 years now,he loved his flat with the location,his dad had come down from london on several occasions when he found the time to visit ashley bringing with him ashleys two younger brothers myles and jaydon both spending a few weekends with him whenever he brought them to Port Talbot.

Ashley walked into his bedroom turned on the lights taking a few gulps of cool water into his mouth from the bottle then placed it onto his pine chest of draw then started taking his jumper off putting it on his double bed then his shirt then vest leaving them all on his bed then he flipped his slippers off took off his trousers leaving it on the bedroom floor then he took both his socks off before putting his feet back into his slippers dressed now only in his pink boxer shorts with purple slippers walking back out into the hallway walking on into his bathroom turning on the bathroom light leaning over the bath turning on the hot water tap to full,his eyes now looking at the shelves on the wall which had two clean towels left on it,leaving the hot water tap running he left the bathroom going back into the bedrooom picking up the bottle of water from his chest of draws,taking a quick sip from it holding onto the bottle while walking out of his bedroom through the upstairs hallway back into the dining room knowing his phone had to be left on charge for a little while before he turned it on walking across the room straight over to the window where his rainbow coloured curtains were widely opened,closing them then looked back at the pile of letters on the sofa before leaving the room walking back into the bathroom seeing the bath water rapidly rising,ashley turned the cold water tap on then slowed down the flow of the hot water tap standing there waiting for a short while watching the cold water gushing from out of the tap filling up the bath tub then eventually started to feel the water temperature to see if it was the right heat for him to take his bath,

mm,he said before turning off both taps taking off his boxer shorts happily climbing into the nice very warm bath water

on the top head of the bath there were a few plastic bottles of shampoo hair conditioner soaps with a lot more in the bathroom cupboard just below the shelf with towels on,he stayed in the bathroom washing himself then relaxing in the warm water relaxed meditating cleaning not just his body but also trying to cleanse his mind from whatever rubbles and clutter was storeds up inside of it.

Now he was back in his dining room with his bathroom towel wrapped around his waist the bath soapy water letting itself flow down the plug hole his boxer shorts still on the bathroom floor as he leaned down near his tv by the plug socket unplugging the charger from his phone walked back to his sofa turned on his phone then left it by his side while his eyes looked towards the tv set at the programme now being shown called,The only way his Essex,it took his mind away from everything for now to watch the programmes on the tv.

.   It was only when he started hearing his miss called with messages coming through on his mobile phone his eyes turned to his phone on the sofa picking it up while the miss calls with text messages were still appearing on the phones screen he started scrolling through his miss calls seeing various peoples names who had been trying to get in contact with him then he scrolled onto his fathers name 3 miss calls with the dates beside it

oh my dad,he said then continued scrolling on through his missed calls then started looking through all the text messages he recieved throughout these missing days finding he also had 2 texts from his dad,he sat there and started to read them then realised after he had finished,his dad had been in Port Talbot knocking on his flat door having been in Port Talbot a few days but was now back in london,Ashley scrolled through his contact until he came to his dads number then called it.

CHAPTER 93
VISITING

Back in London city in the east london area of hackney homerton on chatsworth road where christine lived she was at home in her flat accompanied by three of her daughters charlene asher and niome with son towie and her brother stephen they were all in her living room chatting away.

Stephen had been at his sisters just over a hour after leaving his home in edmonton after speaking to christine telling her he was coming to visit her,she told him her three daughters and son who were there with her.

He took the 149 bus from edmonton green sitting upstairs at the back of the bus on the far left hand side so he could look outside of the bus window while the bus was on it's journey the bus was busy downstairs and upstairs,he watched the passengers getting on and off the bus through the upstairs window also watching the passengers leaving the bus from upstairs also climbing up the stairs of the bus to sit down upstairs.

The bus rolled onwards up the road of White Hart Lane birdy looked out at the new Tottenham football staduim which was only built a short time ago standing there looking fabulous,he remembered not that long ago when he was passing it on the bus watching it slowly getting constructed when the ground work was just getting laid now the ground was fully completed opened to the public,he kept looking out of the bus window wheel the wheels of the bus kept rolling around and around stopping letting people off and on until it eventually stopped at an area known as Seven sisters,birdy's eyes were looking out of the bus window when he spotted Junior standing among the queue of people outside the bus getting on board

surprise surpise,he thought also know while thinking to himself Junior would not be on the bus very long only a few stops because he lived in the next near area known as Stamford Hill,he got up leaving the back seat walking pass the passengers sitting on the left and right of the bus then walked downstairs in search of Junior who he found sitting near the backseat of the bus

alright junior whats up man ?

hay birdy how are you where are you going ? he asked

birdy took the empty seat in the busy bus beside him,

i'm going to hackney to check my sister,

so where you coming from,he asked junior

looking at him with two plastic carrier bags down by his feet i've just come back from brixton when there to buy some fresh meat from my people in the market

one thing birdy knew about junior and this was he was a very good cook,you were guranteed to get a good healthy plate of good food whenever you went to visit him at his home whether it be oxtail and rice or cowfoot with butterbeans goat meat or something on the BBQ in his back garden you name it he sure knew how to put a good plate of food together.

So you are own your way home then birdy asked him knowing he would probably be getting off the bus in a few stops time

birdy hadn't seen junior neither had he spoken to him on the phone for atleast a few weeks so he was pleased to bump into him so whats up with the art exhibitons junior

we will be having another one in a month or two I will let you know the date junior told him

how,s james bond birdy asked with a little laugh,birdy looking at junior,

unior smiled knowing also understanding what birdy meant knowing this was the name they both called james between themselve, james being a older friend of junior's who seem toi have his finger in every legal pie

alright just phone or text me when you get the date,

I will try to make it this time okay,birdy said

Yeah no problem Junior answered now starting to pick up his two plastic bags filled with meat knowing he was moments away from the bus stop he was to get off a,Birdy stood up making room for junior to get up from his seat the bus started to slow down then stop

okay see you soon junior

yeah birdy,junior said now holding his bags walking pass a few seats then followed a few passengers off at the bus stop,birdy stayed on the bus for another three more stops getting off at the Stamford hill area getting another bus which took him near to his sisters home in hackney.

Now here he sat with his sister and his three nieces and nephew who were all now adults the youngest of the three now 25 years old,stephen had left his jacket on the coat hanger in the hallway of the flat among other coats with jackets,there he sat on the sofa charlene sat next to him asher her younger sister sat on a single armchair to the right near the window which looked out onto chatsworth road down below naomi eboe christine's griffin ryan sat on the arm of the armchair next to asher,naomi eboe christine's griffin ryan the youngest of the girls,their mother christine was sitting on the other single armchair to the left of the room ras tau kush stood right by the side of his mother all were lively in talk amongst each other.

Stephen's mobile phone which he was holding in his hand started ringing he looked at it in his hand seeing it was his son ashley's name flashing on the screen

ho it's ashley,he said just before answering the call

he sat there speaking to his son before handing the phone over to ras tau kush to speak to his older first cousin then ras tau kush handed it over to charlene then to asher then naomi eboe christine's griffin ryan

so he could speak to all his first cousin's on aunt christine side of the Birdy family.

CHAPTER.94 ALONE

That same evening back at home in the living room of the house he sat there the tv was on which was the only thing which could be heard in his home while he sat there alone his mind filled up with thoughts as he sat there not even looking at the televison set,his mind was a million miles away from what the tv was showing this present evening.

Last night he went to the hospital having no choice but to go there to get his bottom and top lip stitched up,his lips felt very sore his right eye was swollen with a big black bruise showing beneath it,his nose was also swollen he was lucky feeling very glad to hear the news from the nurse telling him after he had an x-ray it wasn't broken but his jaw on the right side he was told was badly bruised but atleast it weren't fractured .

Before he left the hospital he was given a prescription to collect some strong pain killers from the chemist which he did before going back home washing 2 tablets down with a glass of water about 2 hours ago which seemed to be easing his pain a little bit but still he was filled with aches and pains all over his face.

Right now he felt angry fuming filled up with the spirit of revenge he had been on his mobile phone yesterday evening talking to ching and foxie about what had happened to him after waking up in his home's hallway realising he had been ko'd out then left laying there on his hallway floor covered in his own blood from his bleeding nose with cut lips he struggled getting up on his feet turning on the hallway light staggering to his upstairs bathroom turning on the light looking in his bathroom mirror,shock covered his face when he saw the damage which had been inflicted on his face which was all covered dripping with his blood,he didn't know how long he had been laying there unconscuious,on the hallway floor,he thought while looking in the mirror at his two swollen eyes two thick lips covered in blood and a thick swollen bleeding nose including a swollen aching right jaw,after washing all the blood from his face then holding tissue papers to his two ruined lips which were still bleeding having to keep changing the tissues he phoned foxie first telling him he had been beaten up and robbed by two black dudes who invited themselves into his house,then he phone ching telling him the same thing before saying i've got to go to the hospital I think I need stitches in my both lips.

Ching and foxie met him at the hospital last night the both of them shocked to see the state on curtis's face he looked busted up big time,they stayed at the hospital with him until he got properly cleaned up then surgically stitched up,leaving with him going back to his home with him staying with him all night until the morning listening to all what curtis had to say,I want revenge he was constantly telling his two friends also saying he believed bulla and the dread was behind his attack,it must be something connected to them he told ching and foxie knowing since he had only just stopped doing business with bulla and the dread he has got a home invasion by two black dude who he had never seen in his life,his commonsenses told him the black dudes must be from cardiff knowing to himself that was where most of the blacks in wales came from this was where most of the black people in wales lived. there were hardly any in bridgend for even this town he lived in port talbot had way much more black people than bridgend.

I want revenge he kept saying to ching and foxie sitting there this early morning popping another two more pain killers into his mouth,the three of them sat there in his living room now trying to device a plan in how to get revenge on bulla and the dread.

CHAPTER 95
GOT AWAY

Going back to the night when curtis got robbed and beaten up by ratchet and blazer they both left curtis laying on his hallway floor ko'd out taking his drugs then stepping out of his home closing his front door behind them,they walked down the driveway opened his gate stepped out into the street closing his gate behind them,they both smoothly walked back to the car bulla in the back seat waiting for them ratchet opening the driver door climbed in blazer opened the driver side door climbing in,ratchet handed the black rucksack bag to blazer just as he closed the passenger side door

lets go,bulla said

ratchet started up the car engine then drove out of the street making his way back to the A48 motorway as they all laughed amongst each other

easy money blazer said his hand opening up the rucksack to see if the 3 separate wraps of cocaine was there

there should be 3 ounces in there Bulla said from the back seat

yeah there's 3 ouinces in here Blazer said 1 ounce in each of these wraps

we will weigh them all once we get back to my place bulla said

yeah answered ratchet and blazer

there's an ounce for each of us bulla continued to say as ratchet directed his car now onto the A48 pushing his foot down hard onto the gas pedal allowing the car to pick up speed moving along swiftly in the fast lane switching on the music system filling the car with the musical sounds of the artist singing Coolio's song Gangsters paradise.

CHAPTER 96
THINKING

Back forward to the present evening curtis sat there on his living rooms sofa with his mind filled with thoughts all on his lonesome his tv switched on with him having no interest on what the tv had to offer this evening,he was feeling sore all over his face having no intentions of leaving his home atleast for a few days waiting for his blackeye with swollen right side jaw to go down and heal up,he was feeling at a loss knowing the 3 ounces of cocaine had been stolen from him,it had now knocked him right back next to broke,he now knew he had nothing to trade to all his waiting customers who had been now phoning him for their regular supplies,he also knew the deal would be off with luis until he was able to somehow come up with some sort of cash again.

He was now stuck broke there was only one way he could get back in a position,this was to somehow rob bulla and the dread he had spoken about this matter with ching and foxie earlier this morning before they left his home once I heal up we will set a trap for them he said

okay ching and foxie said before walking through his front door.

The plan they were talking amongst each other was for curtis to somehow win over bulla's confidence of waiting to buy from him again and not to make mention of him being robbed,when bulla and the dread met up hopefully down at the beach front in Port Talbot they will be robbed of their merchandise and beaten up.

That same evening curtis didn't phone luis to tell him what had happened to him because he believed also knowing luis was not involved in any of this fully believing it was all to do with bulla and the dread also he wanted to be careful not letting luis know anything incase somehow luis may tell bulla and the dread,his mind had been filled with thoughts all day since his two friends had left his home,he had been thinking maybe luis does know and was involved with bulla and the dread and he had been set up and they are all laughing at him,no this couldn't be possible he thought because luis would be the one greatly losing out on selling a few ounces every few weeks to him,it would be ridiculous for him to be involved because there would be very little to gain in it for him and a lot more loss,the only one's he could see losing out would be bulla and the dread,he sat there on his sofa that evening in his front room thinking away.